Alpine Apprentice

Alpine Apprentice

SARAH GORHAM

The University of Georgia Press ▲▲▲ *Athens*

Published by the University of Georgia Press
Athens, Georgia 30602
www.ugapress.org
© 2017 by Sarah Gorham
All rights reserved
Designed by Erin Kirk New
Set in 10 on 14 Adobe Caslon Pro
Printed and bound by Thomson-Shore, Inc.
The paper in this book meets the guidelines for
permanence and durability of the Committee on
Production Guidelines for Book Longevity of the
Council on Library Resources.

Most University of Georgia Press titles are
available from popular e-book vendors.

Printed in the United States of America
21 20 19 18 17 P 5 4 3 2 1

Library of Congress Cataloging-in-Publication Data

Names: Gorham, Sarah, 1954– author.
Title: Alpine apprentice / Sarah Gorham.
Description: Athens : The University of Georgia Press, [2017] | Series: Crux:
    the Georgia series in literary nonfiction
Identifiers: LCCN 2016031852 | ISBN 9780820350721 (pbk. : alk. paper) |
    ISBN 9780820350714 (ebook)
Classification: LCC PS3557.O7554 A6 2017 | DDC 814/.54—dc23 LC record
    available at https://lccn.loc.gov/2016031852

In memory of

Natalie Lüthi-Peterson (1927–2012) and

Armin Lüthi (1927–2013)

"Benevolent in the vicinity rises a mountain, and up you go, evenings, climbing delicately looped paths, to gaze down upon the serenity and the splendor, wave a hand, extend an arm in greeting. This town of my love, of my many, many askings, this ribbony lapdog town is my domain."

—ROBERT WALSER

"In speaking of this desire for our own far-off country, which we find in ourselves even now, I feel a certain shyness. I am almost committing an indecency. I am trying to rip open the inconsolable secret in each one of you—the secret which hurts so much that you take your revenge on it by calling it names like Nostalgia and Romanticism and Adolescence."

—C. S. LEWIS

Contents

Preface

Elements of a Recurring Dream

Dorm room that must be clean before departure
Books that will not sit straight
Storage area and unstable ladder to reach it
Suitcase plaid and tattered with broken zipper
Piles and piles of old shirts, blue jeans, summer dresses
Empty hallways suggesting I'm late, the last to go
The feeling that life has frozen around me
The little hotel where I go for help
Phone book with shifting, unreadable print
Swiss Air under *S*, or Special Charter Plane, or is it
    Boat under *B*
Yellow shuttle bus pausing less than three minutes for
    travelers to board
Those punctual Swiss Germans
My wallet, where is my wallet, my passport
Not even one dollar or Swiss franc or rappen (one-hundredth
    of a franc, demonetized in 2007)
Flannel-like social security card
Missing the bus because I'm hauling too much luggage
Missing my mother across the ocean and her black
    cashmere sweater
No other place to go, even without a mother
Don't want to keep a single thing in my luggage anyway
Finally, walking to the airport, dream-fast

No, *leaping*, one ice rectangle to the next
Sorry, all flights out of Switzerland are canceled, indefinitely
There is a boat, less expensive
Ticket collector who accepts my social security card
Even though I'm late
Probable oncoming windstorm, icebergs, tidal wave
Rust splayed across the hull of our ship
Ship that begins its long passage, sailing just above water

Most dreams can be boiled down to a handful of scenarios: being unprepared for a test, falling, flying, appearing naked in public, losing one's teeth, missing a plane, train, bus. They focus on negative feelings—more anger than love, more fear than pleasure—characteristics that cross all cultural boundaries or personality types and arise from experiences everyone has. Experts describe these distillations as "emotional salience." A full orchestra transposed to a single instrument. Surreal juxtapositions of action, sound, and image—all boiling down to . . . anxiety. You need no interpreter to understand that. Somehow, our dreams identify issues that are most important to us, that require further consideration, regardless of what else we might be doing and thinking during the day.

The recurring dream follows a path through the subconscious, like architectural "desire lines." No matter how various the neural pathways, it takes the short cut, the most efficient route. The dream has decided this is the way to go, beginning perhaps in childhood or adolescence, persisting through adulthood and into the golden years with very little change in content, despite a more settled and even-keeled waking life as we approach old age, despite cultural changes that may have occurred over six or seven decades.

I've been dreaming Switzerland for more than forty years. The landscape has dominated my subconscious since 1971, when I took my last flight home out of Zurich as a teenager. It is skipping-record constant, playing out its narrative again and again, with minor variations, night after night. The message is clear—*prepare*. Pack, snack, go to the bank, tune up my ancient Volkswagen, or set my watch to U.S./Switzerland time. In waking life I've transcended the young person jitters (SATS, Heavy Suitcases) and replaced them with mature angst (Poverty in Retirement, Dangerous Spikes in Blood Pressure). And every so often I dream a little progress: I'll abandon the suitcases early, or successfully glide to a stop at Dulles International Airport. But sooner or later my subconscious falters and I slip back into the well-worn night-tracks of my adolescence. Two years in a Swiss boarding school has elongated over my lifetime, a rubber band with no spring back. It is tucked deep into my character, making absolutely clear—though every cell in my body resists this in its constant replenishment—I am still that adolescent, like it or not. Family, profession, and all accomplishments fade to black.

In the late sixties, just shy of fifteen, I attended Gordon Junior High School in Washington, D.C., a short walk up Thirty-Fifth Street from my home on Q. These were years of political unrest, large demonstrations on the Mall, and bussing, all of which heightened the already raucous experience of walking to classes, not to mention the classrooms themselves, chaotic or rigidly sedate, depending on the teacher. I was slated for nearby Western High, another enormous public school where, similarly, a white girl could be mocked for her flat chest, stick legs, and hopeful fishnet stockings, then hauled roughly out of a bathroom stall while doing her business. It had happened to me: my scant seventy-six pounds launched into air by three muscular, fully developed girls, then shoved back onto the toilet, where I trembled for two class periods, making absolutely sure the bullies were gone before safety-pinning my stockings back together again and venturing out.

My unhappiness was a swirl of grit, my mortification so acute, I briefly considered lying down in the middle of the street. Perhaps waiting for a rainy night with poor visibility. Perhaps dressed in camouflaging black leotards and ballet slippers. It would, at least, be an *experience*. There was something attractive in that, a calamity that blows ennui and low-grade fear out of the water and forces the universe to act. A suicide would draw family and friends and enemies to my side in regret and terrible grief. It might be fun, if only I survived to enjoy it.

Instead, I harassed my younger sisters, all four of them. Poked the youngest near her eye with a clothes hanger. Accused the next up of wetting her bed. Teased mercilessly while another practiced the piano. Set up a mock hair salon in the hallway, with chairs and basins, and massaged my sisters' hair with Brylcreem, which heavily coated their scalps even after numerous washings. Mixed up a witch's brew of soy sauce, ketchup, flour, corn oil, Jell-O, pepper, milk, Hawaiian Punch, raisins, and peanut butter, forcing spoonfuls into their mouths till they cried for Mother. I was sent to my attic room as often as possible, but nothing contained my fury at this, yet another form of humiliation, so I leaned over the stair rail and howled till I couldn't speak.

There must have been quiet parental-bedroom-after-dark discussions. Genuine concern that overcrowding had created a hostile situation in local schools. Nervous exhaustion on the home front. Patience tested once, twice—far too often. Siblings suffering. What to do? It was then that an aunt with teenagers of her own stepped in with a thought: An old college roommate named Natalie directed an international school in a small neutral country, far away, over the ocean, over Ireland, England, France, just above a verdant valley known as the Haslital. Here on a mountain terrace sat a cluster of buildings called the Ecole d'Humanité, founded by Paul and Edith Geheeb during World War II.

When the hike seems laborious and inefficient, I clap my arms to my sides, take a running leap, and soar, caped crusader, over valley treetops toward the glittering Rosenlaui Glacier. It's travel without the terror of sheer drops, except the gentle one when I land feet first in the snow. I mingle with this gigantic dramatically textured ice-carpet, infused with every facet and variation of white, not to mention the blues mirroring the great umbrella of sky. The glacier smells of metal with a trace of anise. Soon I'm reaching into my pocket to find blueberry lozenges wrapped in cellophane and lo, a Popsicle that leaves my tongue blue stained. This is sustenance for the moment, for a few days even, and I begin trekking over the glacier's angular humps and ridges. The very thought of crevasse brings me perilously close to the edge of a bottomless one, the danger terrific. Before long I'm tumbling headfirst. No room to spread my wings. No grabbing onto handholds. The sky contracts into a baby-blue chevron.

Long ago, dream content was considered revelatory, encompassing far more than primal human emotion. Citizens of the Chinese province Fujian slept on graves in order to receive dream messages from their ancestors. Ancient Mesopotamians believed dreams were mantic, containing clues to the future. Egyptians constructed temples to their male god of dreams, Serapis, where priests served as professional dream interpreters. Pharaohs were indelibly linked to deities; their dreams were considered divine. Twenty-one dreams described in the Bible convey celestial knowledge, specific instructions, and ominous warnings. Some cultures still use their dreams to enter other realities, including the afterlife. Now scientists look to the brain for explanation. MRI scans have revealed that logic and orientation areas of the brain are suppressed during sleep. J. Allan Hobson proposed that when we dream of flight our brain is trying to resolve how we could be physically active when in fact we are in bed, lying stock-still. Others, like George Lakoff and Mark Johnson, see a link to figurative language, as in the metaphors "off to a flying start" and "floating through life."

I prefer an explanation I heard long ago, which pairs nocturnal flight with those ecstatic leaps into the air when mom or dad tossed us high above their heads, swung us around, and (hopefully) returned us safely to the ground.

Suppose you are fifteen and your family made you an offer you couldn't refuse: three years in a mountain paradise, an exotic secondary education no one else your neighborhood would ever have—quick uptake of a brand-new language, skiing, hiking, the best chocolate in the world, coed dorms, and small classrooms. You feel honored by their faith in you, their certainty that you are capable of this undertaking. You'll be traveling alone, forced to navigate German, even Swiss German, for the simplest of tasks. And perhaps most formidable of all to a teenager— you'll be a stranger among strangers, obliged to forge new friendships, while the old ones inevitably wither away.

The alternatives are grim: continued scuffles with four siblings for a scrap of parental attention. Western High School up the street with more cruelty, lazy teachers, boisterous classrooms, even drugs—hard drugs. You say yes. Yes, Mama. Yes, Daddy. That would be great.

In your ninth-grade yearbook, there's a little blank space under each student's photo for life goals: to be a hairdresser, a mechanic, politician, or mathematician. Scuba diving in the Bahamas.

Yours? *To go to Switzerland.* This is no dream. It's actually happening: a see-you-later-alligator thumb-in-the-eye of all sisters and tough girls of the past, present, and future.

Success guaranteed.

Alpine Apprentice

How to Get There

The modern carry-on, with multidirectional wheels and retractable handle, is decades away. All you have is what's available, circa 1968, in the creepy attic of your parents' house—an enormous Scotch plaid, canvas-sided suitcase and an olive-green army duffel, though your father avoided the draft, thanks to asthma and a bad back. You've been sent a list of necessities, and it's all stacked on your bed in neat piles: two blankets (a down comforter can be rented for a fee), favorite pillow, three sets of sheets and towels (Mom buys matching sets in yellow, rose, and blue), winter *and* summer clothes, hiking boots, Converse All Stars, Wallabees, dress shoes, sandals, down jacket, three months' worth of toiletries, pencils and pens, stationery, art supplies, and so on.

Your dresser drawers are nearly empty, with the exception of those orphaned socks, their mates long gone to rags or just plain gone. The closet bursts with sundresses you'll never wear and irreplaceable costumes from your youth. Here's a tutu with pink sequins edging the tulle. A queen's royal cape in gold satin rolled into a ball. Not to mention shoeboxes full of fake necklaces and your precious collection of trolls. How to favor one thing over another, say farewell to the scorned and abandoned?

Just pray the stitchery holds. Luckily, Dad supplies a strap for the suitcase and rope for the duffel, while demonstrating a fine Eagle Scout knot just to be sure. Hefts them onto the bathroom scale—altogether, eighty pounds.

Flight booked by travel agent, gray-green passport with gold lettering tucked inside a brand-new leather billfold big enough to hold

1961 Rambler
Cross Country
Wagon.

dollars *and* francs. Lunch bag with smoked turkey on white bread, apple, and chips. Your parents shiver in the predawn hallway. Upstairs, four sisters snore or talk in their sleep, oblivious. The front door stands open, Thirty-Fifth Street deserted. Somewhere a wrought-iron gate clatters.

Dad boosts the duffel, suitcase, and carry-on knapsack into the Rambler's spacious trunk. Mom in her blue cotton nightie shuffles forward, half-asleep, arms extended. One hand holds a silver ring with turquoise stone, all yours, and yours only. The other pushes you firmly away.

From Washington's National Airport, take any shuttle to New York's Kennedy, where you will wait four hours for the $125 People-to-People charter to Copenhagen. Boarding is first-come-first-serve, and there's no guarantee of a seat if the flight is overbooked. So even though it's rude, muscle your way toward the head of the line. Just before takeoff, cross your arms, legs, every finger possible, and finally, both thumbs. This will ensure a safe lift into air and flight over the very wide ocean known as the Atlantic. Repeat prior to landing or if the plane experiences turbulence during passage.

Ten hours later, the squeal and jolt of touchdown signals a temporary pause to your anxiety. On to baggage claim. Though you checked your luggage this far, from now on you will have to carry everything yourself. The customs officer squints at your passport, curious perhaps that you are wearing wire-, not plastic-rimmed, glasses, as in the photo. Or maybe this is merely his official scowl and no traveler is spared. You have an eight-hour layover. Stash your bags in two lockers. Rest up for the next leg of the journey by grabbing a nap on the grassy riverbank outside Tivoli Gardens. The waters flow brownish and thick. Other citizens sunbathe here and there. A shadow passes over your face, and you wake to the sight of an old man, hand scratching his butt, eyes fastened on your chest. No one else is around.

Soon you will begin a twenty-hour train ride to Zurich. Though you've purchased a couchette, the conductor does not like Americans, especially *teenage* Americans, and leads you to a second-class compartment instead, where the seats do not extend fully and are constructed of stiff leather, now sweat stained. Intimate grazing of stranger body parts is inevitable, sleep impossible. Expect to enter a kind of strung exhaustion with no concentration as you turn page after page of your book. The stench of garlic and beer is crushing, and a woman lays her hand on your knee, but with a porter's help, you finally alight in Zurich's Hauptbahnhof, where life appears to be cool, punctual, and full of echoes. Purchase a one-way ticket with its stack of destinations: Schweiz, Bernese Oberland, Brünig-Hasliberg, and finally Goldern, like the tiniest Russian nesting doll. Do try a bratwurst for sale at one of any number of open-air vendors. It may be your best bratwurst ever. Point to a slightly charred one and open your hand with several Swiss francs catching the early sun.

Welcome to the Swiss *Schnellzug*. Trains swoop in a few minutes before departure, unload, load, swoop out again. They move silently over the tracks, doors responding to a tug of the handle and whisking open and closed. Make sure to board early in the no-smoking cars, position forward, unless of course you prefer like Proust (your mother's favorite) to travel time in reverse.

SBB! Oh, how we love thee. Her wheels are equipped with balancers, and there's extra soundproofing so that the lady travels smooth, zipping down the tracks as if dressed in sateen. You could grab a few winks after the sleepless flight over, then the long ride from Denmark, but *don't you dare*, for the scenery is too lovely to sleep through. To the right, a small *Wiese* with grazing sheep; to the left, an electrical plant. Yes, the Swiss need their lights and washing machines too. Not far beyond the city, mountains begin to appear in the distance, snow-sifted and smudged with a bit of gray haze. The train stops briefly at Zug, population twenty-seven thousand. The *Zug* passes through Zug and continues humming along a triplet of aquamarine lakes or perhaps one long lake that dives below ground, resurfacing for your touristic pleasure. Everywhere on steep hillsides stand clusters of white stucco houses with orange tile roofs, some quite close to the tracks, arranged the way a nice little girl might arrange her toys. One needn't fear any-thing on this train—no terrible delays, no accidents. The train slows to let another train pass, which, *natürlich*, is on schedule.

There's an hour layover in Lucerne, lovely medieval city by the lake, perfect for a walk to the harbor for the city's most flattering profile of domicile, steeple, and swish-swashing waters. Oh, that water: brilliant blue-green, whiff of ice and mint and skiing. It's early yet to practice your very elementary German, but you don't want to board the wrong coach, so you try, piecing a question together before a railroad man, just as your mother instructed:

"*Wo fährt der Zug nach Brünig, bitte?*"

"*WAS?*" he snarls. "*WAS?*"

"*Wo ist der Zug nach Brünig, bitte?*" Mmm, *Gleis*. That's it. "*Welche, uh, welcher Gleis nach Brünig, bitte?*"

"*Ahhh! Acht, Gleis acht.*" Track eight.

This train is more rough and tumble, creeping closer and closer to the mountains with their toothed summits and saddles spotted with melting snow. This carriage rocks, throwing bags into the aisle and passengers against doorframes. Riverside! A man on his white horse! Is that someone famous? An Italian family climbs aboard—two children, mother and father, and grandma. The little girl counts to ten. Again. Again. The boy plays with the window, bang slide thud. Their language has cloying tones. Alas, they are counterpoint to your pleasure, nudg-ing and poking with nonstop effusiveness.

The engineer locks in the climbing gear. The train staggers forward and begins in earnest to ascend. *Verboten* to open windows fully wide and now you know why, for rock face and telephone poles are scarcely a foot from your face, stuck out to catch the breeze and watch the foremost cars snake around a bend. But it's irresistible, that breeze. Velvety hillsides and, again, those lakes the hue of emeralds before they're polished. A woman steps forward from the opposite seat and, leaning over your lap, lifts the window with a harrumph. The ticket collector rumbles behind in rough *Hochdeutsch*: "*Bitte die Fenstern nicht öffnen! Besonders in Tunneln!*"

Then Lungern, finally Brünig, and it's time to disembark. The PostBus idles near the road, its departure imminent, allowing a slim five minutes for passengers to run across the railway platform with suitcases, rucksacks, and ski equipment. Board here and mention your stop. The bus's hydraulics kick in with a groan, like an old dog rising off the floor, and the door shivers shut. Off you go through seventy-foot pine forests, around hairpin curves, under tunnels carved into the rock—just wide enough for the bus, but hardly an oncoming car. Look down, or don't. Guardrails made of rusted steel are more like handrails, thin and not quite two feet high. Lip service, really, when it comes to a vehicle as enormous as this. Tough to travel in a car that overheats easily or has sketchy brakes. No place to pull over and raise your hood, even less room for error. Imagine that long tumble down, slowed perhaps, but not arrested, by those evergreens. In one village, a second-story porch juts into the street, forcing the driver to slow. He passes with centimeters to spare, not a shingle displaced or railing splintered. You don't see a whole lot of bent fenders either, so common on U.S. streets. Surely the Swiss have their accidents, but like those ants in farms we used to jiggle in their green frames, if you disrupt their surroundings, they immediately set about fixing them.

As the bus rounds blind corners, it sounds its horn in a French police car trio of notes. The driver has adorable cheeks like Winnie-the-Pooh and a delicate, ski-jump nose. This is one traveler's lesson: Trust him. He knows what he's doing. Get yourself to the bus stop on time and the driver will do the rest.

"*Goldern! Ecole d'Humanité!*" Your signal to hop off. The teddy bear assisted you before, and kindly does so again, digging into the storage compartment and throwing both bags at your feet.

Footsteps

The Ecole d'Humanité has developed, almost in its entirety and down to the smallest details, from a single, essential thought: Become who you are. *This process of "becoming" begins on a student's very first day, which is usually a time of radical reorientation. When choosing morning and afternoon courses, or a project for the Intensive Week, or a hike or skiing tour, or Ecole family, students are continually challenged with the question "What do I want? What do I really want?" And when difficulties arise, they do not lead automatically to decisions made by committees of adults. They lead, rather, to critical discussions centering on the question "Who do I want to be?" allowing people to hone their individuality at the same time as they find their place in a community: this is the school's central mission.*

Long ago there lived an idealistic man named Paul Geheeb, born 1870 in a pharmacy in Geisa, Germany. He married the far more practical Edith Cassirer, born 1885, and the two became leaders in an early progressive educational movement, which flowered in the late nineteenth and early twentieth centuries. Of particular interest were the *Landerziehungsheime* (progressive boarding schools), located in the country, far from the harmful influences of the big cities. Their practices were holistic, based on the ideas of John Locke, Thomas Arnold, Michel de Montaigne, and Jean-Jacques Rousseau.

Thanks to Edith's father, Max Cassirer, a wealthy lawyer, the Geheebs were able to design and construct their dream school in 1910—the Odenwaldschule in southwestern Germany. The school was coeducational and democratic. Students set up rules for the community, cleaned the buildings, selected their own courses, evaluated their own progress, and devoted a significant amount of time to artistic, athletic, and socially noteworthy activities. It thrived for twenty years under Paul and Edith's direction. Others would follow over the years with similar intentions—large educational systems like Waldorf (1919) and smaller schools like England's Summerhill (1921), to name two.

On March 7, 1933, Nazis acted on rumors that the Odenwaldschule was a "communist Jew school" and invaded the small village of Heppenheim. They arrived at the main building, brandishing guns, herding all two hundred students and faculty into the auditorium, where they ordered the "communists" to stand up and hand in their literature. No one moved, so the soldiers ransacked the property and found a few pamphlets. Encouraged, the Nazis demanded more. In his book *The Politics of Progressive Education*, Dennis Shirley describes the scene: "The students fanned out and brought back the books they thought the Nazis wanted. After a stay of more than two hours, the storm troops departed, carrying off copies of Marx's *Capital*, travel books about Russia, literature on coeducation, chemistry books with suspiciously red covers, and a Sanskrit dictionary—which they mistook for Hebrew." What followed were a full year of Nazi control and the near destruction of all progressive educational policies. Edith and Paul had no choice but to flee to Switzerland, along with just twenty-four children.

More than four locations failed and ten extraordinarily difficult years passed before they settled in Goldern. At their first point of exile in Versoix, near Geneva, Paul named his small group of emigrants School of Humanity or Ecole d'Humanité, a "vigorous and humanistic *action*" in response to national Socialism. There were problems from the start. Students had to learn French. A Russian boy was held at the border between Germany and Switzerland, under suspicion his parents might be communists. And one morning, a student climbed up on an unsecured stack of logs, set it rolling, and was quickly crushed. It was the Ecole's first casualty and many decades would pass before they faced another, long after Paul and Edith had died.

At their second location they occupied Schloss Greng, a largely unwinterized castle near Lake Murten, which also served as a barracks. In the fall, Paul wrote: "I freely admit that our immediate existence is hideous. We have two hundred soldiers and another twenty officers and their subordinates. They have taken the classrooms and the few heated rooms. . . . On top of this I have so much work and don't have the time continually to do gymnastics to warm up. . . . But the attitude of the children is beautiful, truly heroic. From the oldest to the youngest they work for our project and give their best. Nonetheless, at least a half dozen are now ill with cold."

That winter was unbearable, so the Geheebs moved their school to an abandoned hotel near the Schwarzsee, south of Bern. There they faced financial ruin. Only nine students remained, all of them refugees, many "shattered and perhaps psychologically destroyed forever." But as time passed, thanks to the Swiss Assistance Agency for Emigrant Children, more and more children were sent to the Ecole with stipends, and by 1944 the school was bursting at the seams. Shirley described the situation: "sixty *Kameraden* . . . lived in the huts and cabins surrounding Schwarzsee. The conditions were so crowded that some of the Kameraden entered and left their rooms through their windows rather than the door so that every inch of floor space could be used for bedding. The students who prepared meals had to be especially quiet so as not to disturb the students who were attending class a few yards away in the dining room."

A bit of luck came their way in when *Life* magazine printed a feature with several photographs of Geheeb and his students. The short text reads:

> On the shores of LacNoir near Zürich, Switzerland, a crowded little school, aptly called Ecole d'Humanité, stands as an oasis in the desert of European education. Here 40 young pupils are taught the lessons of reason and tolerance by a 75-year-old German educator named Paulus Geheeb. . . . More philosopher than businessman, Geheeb is now in danger of losing his school for lack of funds because the majority of the students are refugees from all over Europe who are unable to pay tuition.

Paul Geheeb, with
young student at the
Ecole d'Humanité,
Schwarzsee, 1946.

Boys dormitory,
Schwarzsee, 1946.

Three thousand dollars in donations arrived in the mail, roughly thirty-six thousand dollars in today's dollars—a surprisingly small amount for such significant publicity.

In 1946, Paul and Edith traveled to the Hasliberg in the Bernese Oberland and discovered the village of Goldern, an ideal new location for their school. Initially town authorities rejected their application—they feared the negative influences on their quiet hamlet—but canton authorities overruled. At last, the Geheebs had found a permanent home for their school.

When I arrived in 1969, Paul Geheeb had been dead for eight years, but his legacy was golden. Portraits hung in offices, library, and auditorium—he was a godly man without whom the Odenwaldschule and its offspring the Ecole would not exist. Known to many as Paulus (Saint Paul), he'd been awarded the Goethe plaque from the German Ministry of Science, Education, and Culture, as well as honorary doctorates from Tübingen and Visva-Bharati universities. He was even a candidate for the Nobel Peace Prize in 1952.

Paulus worked on the third floor of *Haupthaus*, one of the oldest buildings on the Ecole's campus, with a warren of dark hallways and bleak overhead lighting. His office was painstakingly maintained, guarded by a sign—*No messes in Paulus's study! No food or trink!* It was both community and sacred space. Everyday meetings took place at the round table and visiting researchers also sat here flipping the thin, dried-out pages of letters dating back to the 1940s, collected in pale blue folders called *Mappen*. His possessions were arranged as in a gallery, the oak rolltop desk laden with miniature, framed photographs, souvenirs, and carvings, including a small statue of Buddha. A green-tiled, Dutch-style stove stood in one corner, propped up on cinderblocks. Ancient leather-jacketed editions of German literature were jammed into bookshelves lining two walls. And framed portraits of famous men hung on the walls: Nietzsche with his monstrous mustache, Beethoven, Einstein, and a glowering Dostoevsky, beard splayed across his chest. On the south wall, a row of single-hung windows looked out over the Engelhorn and Wetterhorn mountains—a quite incredible view. Each window was fronted with a casement and to the

Paul Geheeb and students.

door was hitched a second, heavier door, conserving energy, protecting against fire, or keeping the secrets in.

Here is an oft-reproduced photograph, prominent in the school's brochure.

White-haired and long-bearded, cross-legged on a log, balancing in his right hand a pair of reading glasses, Paul is surrounded by six youngsters, who are following his words closely. Have they been coached, posed, enticed with chocolate to be still and listen? His pale calves are visible, as he has rolled his pants to the knee and the shoes he's wearing oddly resemble Mary Janes. He's at home in the country, comfortable inside the semicircle of kids. What nugget of wisdom holds them so rapt? Gifted with the ability to abstract the many infuriating details of a child's education and transform it into an elegant theory, wasn't it true he spoke most thrillingly to parents, educators, the ether? I couldn't imagine the scene wasn't staged. Surely there was a shadow version somewhere in the files. The kids were simply behaving as instructed, right? That kind of default cynicism was typical of a self-centered, disrespectful American teenager.

Later, I heard that Edith was the go-to half of the founding couple, the one with her feet on the ground who jiggered theory into practice and took actual steps to resolve their many issues. She was equally revered and lived just three years short of a hundred. During my residency, a solo audience with Edith was rare though she was not at all intimidating—warm, heavy, and amiable in her old-fashioned housedress, the definition of *matronly* in the best sense of that word. She offered Nescafé and butter biscuits and was concerned how well her visitors were adjusting to life in the Ecole. She motioned me in, a new arrival, patted her shawl-covered ottoman, and asked in accented English whether I was happy. I saw immediately she knew more of my short history than I cared to admit, though with Edith, I kept my responses polite and unrevealing. I inhaled her cookies like a starving person.

Edith Geheeb
with students.

In 1948, two formidable young people joined the Ecole as interns. The first was Swiss musician Armin Lüthi. Having completed his *Matura*, and realistic about his talent as violinist, he'd signed up for teacher training at the Oberseminar, Zurich. Only a few weeks in, he contracted TB and began a ten-month stay at a Beatenberg sanitarium. This kept him from his studies but also from military service. Once healthy, he was able to return to Zurich, picking up where he left off with prerequisites in education, as well as courses in music, mechanics, sports, and drawing. Here's where he first heard mention of *Landerziehungsheimen*. Geheeb's Ecole d'Humanité came up in the conversation too, though not in a particularly flattering light. Colleagues inside the school had heard tales of poverty and disruption and all agreed, "This school and its teacher(s) are totally impossible." Armin nevertheless made the decision to pursue his *Praktikum* in Goldern. A massive teacher shortage had followed the war and because of the tremendous exigency, he felt both obliged and curious.

Then came Natalie Peterson, graduate of Wellesley College with a degree in German, part-time teacher at the Odenwaldschule. She planned to spend some time researching her dream project, an international summer camp known initially as Young Leaders International. A colleague suggested, "You ought to go up on the Hasliberg—there's a man there who has ideas similar to yours." She drove up to Goldern, where she met the Geheebs. Later, Edith asked if she could have a ride to the valley village of Meiringen. On the way down the brakes gave and they were forced to spend the night while the car was repaired. Edith was very thankful and sorry of course that the car broke down, so she said: "If you ever would like to work here, please let me know." Natalie thought it over and agreed the school might be a good place to begin work on the camps while pursuing a *Praktikum*.

Her first take on the Ecole? At the tail end of winter, a letter to her mother, dated April 1949:

> The surroundings are of a cold and granite-like beauty. Mountains rise on all sides, covered with snow, and with a glacier crawling icily down one. Below the fields are very green and covered with flowers and neat little peasants' houses. It's very different from the Odenwald, where the

hills are sweet and gentle and there are woods everywhere. I can't love it much here yet, but maybe I will before I leave. The kids are different, too. Wilder, not so well disciplined as the orderly little Germans, and terribly impolite. Maybe they're both extremes, but the OSO was easier to take. The children I have aren't bad, but you don't have the feeling that they're excited about learning the way you do in the OSO. . . . I'm awfully homesick for Heppenheim as you may have noticed.

Armin and Natalie met during Natalie's first year and very soon became a couple, the high point in what was a chaotic period of their lives. After two years, they fled to Basel, where Armin worked at a city orphanage and later became director at the Waldschule Pfeffingen, a boarding school for adolescents with behavioral and learning disorders. The salary was better than expected and for the first time in his life, he could pay back his debts. They had their own vineyard and lived in a lovely neighborhood with "nice baroque bourgeois houses." But Natalie was bored, and anyway, it wasn't long before Edith begged them to return as full-time teachers. The school's financial situation was precarious. Out of forty children only a few were able to pay tuition, and Armin, because he was the only trained teacher, was one of the best-paid employees at a hundred francs a month (his boots cost 115 francs).

The spring of 1956 brought a massive influx of American student applications. The dollar was worth roughly 4.25 Swiss francs, thus the Ecole presented a cheap alternative to U.S. public and private boarding schools. Natalie saw an urgent need, so she established the American program, which satisfied college prep requirements and allowed students to stay on for at least three years. They could have filled the place with these kids but kept American enrollment to 30 percent, for an international focus was a high priority.

I was among those thirty-five students who benefited from the exchange rate when tuition and room and board set parents back a modest $800, plus the price of a round-trip international flight. We traveled from California, Arizona, Massachusetts, Washington State, Maryland, and Virginia. We'd heard about the Ecole from grandparents, aunts or uncles, friends, anyone associated with the place or its first incarnation in Heppenheim. K.C., for example, was the youngest of four brothers, born in Vienna, though he'd lived all over the place—Berlin, Munich, finally D.C. His father, Russell, had attended the Odenwaldschule in the early 1930s and was present, in fact, on that fateful day Nazi thugs invaded the OSO for the first time, rounding up students like goats, burning their books. While researching educational options for his own children, Russell heard about an internationally famous, radically alternative boarding school in Switzerland "run by an old man with a long white beard." He knew exactly what and whom they were talking about and enrolled his oldest son, Phillip, in 1958. K.C. visited his brother in 1960. He vaguely remembered deep snow, fairy tale houses with shutters, glowing yellow light, and a steep staircase that seemed to disappear into the sky. But he was only five. By fourteen, it was his turn to attend the school.

There was also my cousin Charlie, who worked as Natalie's secretary. His brother Dick attended the school and became fast friends with Creighton, who was Natalie's best friend's son. Mark lived close to Creighton and wound up a student too. Nancy's daughter Busy worked at the school at one point and, decades later, sent over her youngest, Molly. All of us boarded the train to Brünig with children from Israel, Norway, India, Sweden, Denmark, Holland, Japan, and Argentina. The newcomers, jet-lagged and slightly nauseous, held onto their seats, swaying with each brake and lunge, while Swiss boys swaggered and preened, tearing into each other with fake punches. What was this guttural, phlegmy sound issuing from their lips? What were we doing here? That first night we fell into a kind of coma, or hardly slept at all. In less than six months, we'd transition into this remote, tightly knit community, on a mountain 7,365 feet above sea level.

When Paulus died, the board of directors appointed Edith, along with Armin and Natalie, to run the school. Following Edith's death in 1982, the Lüthis remained directors for many decades, and even after retirement continued their close involvement with the Ecole. Since then, several leadership configurations have been in charge, including a team of directors known as *Die Leitung*, dividing their duties into the German-speaking system, the American system, the outdoor/athletic program, financial oversight, and more. The Ecole population has grown to 150 young people, from infants (whose parents work in the school) to a twenty-two-year-old Chinese woman preparing for university. Twenty-five countries are represented, girls and boys in equal proportion, from every economic stratum—financially strapped to exorbitantly wealthy. Despite shockingly low salaries and precious little time off, many faculty and staff remain devoted for years, sometimes a lifetime. This is one reason the Ecole continues to thrive. And most of Geheeb's concepts have proved to be fundamentally alive, attractive, and lasting—more than eighty years—with just a few adjustments to suit the times.

Twenty-Four Hours in the Village of Goldern

It's pitch dark, deep winter, one hour before the sun begins its climb from the east, over Käserstatt, spilling down steep hillsides into the village of Goldern, finally touching on the nest of chalet-style buildings called the Ecole d'Humanité. Newer dorms Ost and Westhaus are perched hillside, concrete and pine, with huge casement windows. Below sit the older structures, outbuildings Baracke and Stöckli, and dorms Haupthaus, Turmhaus, and Waldhaus. These date from an age when surrounding forests, which had to be cleared for meadow and farm, provided the building material. Shingles and siding are weathered to a dark chocolate brown. In the whirling center of the campus sits the multi-use-but-chiefly-for-dining Max Cassirer Haus, also in the newer style, and right next to it, inexplicably, a small round of pasture owned by a village farmer, still grazed by a cow or two, or occasionally a goat.

A few dim bulbs burn over welcome mats, and the cook is stacking old-fashioned milk tins behind the kitchen. Otherwise, there's little sign of life. Even a brooklet slipping over rock seems subdued by the chill and absence of light. The day commences.

▲▲▲ 6:30 a.m.

We stress physical fitness without undue emphasis on competitive sports. Climbing, hiking, swimming, and skiing are some of the activities offered.

No need to set your alarm. A student (usually the mischievous ones like Norbert or Hans or Rüdi) entrusted with waking the entire community will stride through the halls striking a huge brass gong. This is no gentle awakening. The boys take pleasure in lingering by certain doors and striking the metal with wide-open aggression. Light sleepers know when it's coming; the nearly comatose suffer the worst shock, poor souls. And everyone will tumble out of bed, grope in the dark for their T-shirts and shorts, cram into their sneakers, and head outside for obligatory *Morgensport* on the tarmac led by Herr Urs Gabriel. The ground may be packed with snow or cleared off and dry. The man is well over six feet, athletic and handsome, his face dimpled and cheerful, but no one is watching, eyes glazed with exhaustion and sleepy-seeds. Urs is gentle with his troops, though he insists on knee bends, jumping jacks, and touch-your-toes at the very least for a minimum of fifteen minutes. His efforts are valiant with bodies so half-hearted and stiff-limbed. The only truly fit fellow is Urs.

Drag your unlaced sneakers through a thin layer of frost, and bump your way up the dorm's exterior stairs toward your room on the third floor. No light on the mountains just yet though there's a metallic whiff in the air, the smell of ice? Again, you're out of breath, snorting larger and larger plumes of smoke, and you're weak-kneed without breakfast. Not a pleasant feeling. There's worse to come. Throw on your robe and threadbare towel and head back down, this time using the inside steps (two sets, in case of fire). Join the queue filing into a cinderblock basement for *kalte Duschen*—cold showers, the ultimate lesson in personal hygiene and necessary economy, considered by all to confer immunities. Hot water is available only on Sundays, unless you are a lucky *Mitarbeiter* with access to the hidden hot water key. Girls to the left, boys to the right. Various strategies include a quick duck in and out without soap, faking it, though you'd better be sure no one's watching, and yelping to let them know how painful this is in full-throated, horror-movie screams. Truth be told, there are no secrets for enduring a barely above-freezing shower in below-freezing conditions. Just hurry.

Fruhstück in the *Speisesaal*, a large, windowed room with twenty Formica tables and chairs that chafe noisily against the tile floor. Here you'll sit with two teachers, one helper perhaps, and a dozen students of all ages. It's not necessarily company you'd hang with, but at least you have the choice of brown bread with jam and butter over watery porridge. Alas, there's no such thing as toast here. Try mixing the strawberry confit into the oatmeal, which turns it sweet and pink and more palatably thick. Cocoa is poured from communal pitchers into white ceramic bowls. Alas, it's lukewarm. Eating, you'll find, occurs at supersonic speed. Hardly enough time to chew, much less reach for seconds. Before you know it, someone announces, "*Zusammenstellen!*" Dump your leftovers into a tin bowl and pile up your dishes for removal by Service, a gang of upperclass students who balance huge towers of plates and move at an impressive clip on their zigzag paths to the kitchen.

They return with buckets of potatoes for communal potato peeling and slicing in small, medium, or large chunks (wait for instructions). Thus, it is possible to predict at this early hour what you can expect for lunch: boiled, mashed, or less often, home-fried potatoes. Knives are intentionally dull, though codirector Armin pulls from his pocket an ancient Swiss Army knife and rips through his allotment with far too much relish. If *he* loves to peel potatoes, *you* must love to peel potatoes. A chalky residue will remain on your hands so line up single file at the sink to wash it off.

Next: *Ansagen*, or daily announcements, in both Hochdeutsch and English for the sake of the newcomers. David Matson, an overaggressive American with a shock of blond hair and Cro-Magnon jaw, does the honors. It's his moment of glory and everyone flinches a little when he stands up. "*Abwasch, bitte raus kommen*" (Dishwashers, please come out!). "*Bitte die Servietten raus den Tasche nehmen und im schoene Ordenung an dem Tische legen*" (Please take your napkins out of their pouches and place them on the table in an orderly fashion). "There will be no folk dancing until the record player can be repaired. Please do not leave your belongings on the dining hall steps. While you are walking between buildings, pick up at least one piece of trash and dispose of it properly. Congratulations to Walter, who has successfully completed the international baccalaureate."

Swiss boys between the ages of seven and twelve do the best imitation of David in gutturally explosive hacking and far-flung saliva spray.

▲▲▲ 7:30 a.m.

The community is nourished by the fact that students take on a great number of responsibilities that are necessary for its functioning.

Putzpause (obligatory), where all members of the community pause to scour their surroundings, each with specific tasks, the schedule arranged by a pair of trusted students. High in status are meal-related positions such as Service. The cook (Herr Wiessman) is a six-foot wild man with a vicious temper, but gaining his good favor means extra apples or slices of forbidden cheese with white bread. Most other chores are midlevel, anything from scrubbing down hallways with a stinky *Lappen* (rag) to sweeping porches to clearing garden plots to babysitting for the codirectors' daughter, nicknamed Doey.

Toilet duty is reserved for a problem kid or, perversely, the high and mighty. As might be guessed, neither is thorough. Slip slop with rags slung by the tips of their shoes, blobs of bacteria hitting the floor. As you are now fully aware, the school runs on a tight budget and for that reason favors undyed, unbleached toilet paper, the texture of party streamers. *Good for you* is the overall thinking. Toughens a child up. In truth, it wasn't so very long ago (midsixties) that Swiss *Verdingkinder* or "contract children" were torn from their financially struggling families and used as cheap labor on farms. Fortunately, Switzerland has moved beyond that.

So relax. Delinquent scrubbers are rarely left to their own devices: Real live *Helferinnen* (Dutch, Swedish, or English helpers), who value a year off before college even though they are paid virtually nothing, follow up with super keen vision. They make it right, at peace

WC Ente or
Toilet Duck®,
lavender scent.

with Swiss standards of cleanliness. Think of Zurich's airport with its immaculate stalls, floor-to-ceiling doors, and deadbolts that latch shut with a firm click. No sight of your neighbor's shoes or sound of their elimination. A cleaning woman waits quietly outside to make sure your compartment is all set for the next traveler. In local hotels, pristine stalls are wood paneled, with light streaming from high frosted-glass windows. They are warm and private, their locks declaring in bright red letters *besetzt*, or green, *frei*. No one would dare knock; the question of vacancy is not even worth asking.

Speaking of clean, it was the Swiss who invented the "toilet duck": a swan-necked plastic bottle filled with cleaning fluid that makes it amazingly easy to apply cleaner up under the rim.

▲▲▲ 8:30 a.m.

Break for students, time to wash hands, gather up books, or do last-minute homework. For faculty, a quick meet known as the *Mini-Konferenz*. The accordion door in the Speisesaal is pulled shut and fastened tight. An agenda is scribbled on the blackboard in the following order: *Krank* (sick), *Arzt* (doctor), or *Gefehlt* (missing from class), with a short list of names under the headings. At least two adults weigh in on each, occasionally with diverging points of view. Then the reminder that fresh air will do wonders for most of these illnesses, "*Geh doch in die frische Luft!*"

If the weather cooperates, and teachers are in accord, classes may be canceled for a *Ski Tag,* cause for immense celebration. Outside, on the Sportplatz, anticipation builds, for the weather couldn't be better. Kids mill about waiting for the verdict, poking sticks into snowdrifts, flinging snowballs that burst midair. Excellent powder. The sky's blinding sunlight bounces off the white into young faces. One boy tiptoes back into the dining hall, where everything looks purple. He presses his ear to the divider. The latch twitches.

Will it be time to tear off to dorm rooms, change to ski pants and tights, long johns and bell-bottoms, ski socks and thick red wool socks over those, layers of cotton, polyester long-sleeved T-shirts, windbreaker? Time for the scramble with skis and poles and the difficult choice which group to join: beginner, advanced beginner, intermediate, expert? When the decision comes down, will you seek out the novices and ever-so-tender Herr Haas, who brightens with the slightest blip of progress. Or will you risk it and go for the stem Christie group? Something to think about. For other kids, advanced is a no-brainer; they take to the sport with zeal. K.C., for one. By the end of his first winter in Goldern, this fourteen-year-old parallels with the cool guys, wedeling alongside experts, who advise him to *attack* the snow with each turn. After two more seasons, he masters powder and even *jumping* on the slopes he's familiar with.

So what will it be—notebooks and textbooks tossed, last-minute runs to the bathroom, the long walk uphill to Twing, past the Gletscherblick, skis propped onto poles and crossed behind necks, boots stiff and heavy? You're ready with chocolate and a shriveled tangerine tucked into your sweatshirt pocket, just in case. Always a little low on blood sugar. Lots of heavy breathing till you reach the *Gondelbahn* and ride up up up to the top of the winter world. . . .

Ski day? Yes? Yes?

Alas. Proposal shot down. Too much catching up to do in math and history and English.

▲▲▲ 9:00 a.m. to 12:30 p.m.

In Switzerland there are 26 school systems with 26 unique curricula. Here we invent a 27th for Hans and a 28th for Feli.

Classes (obligatory) begin, three in number, fifty-five to seventy-five minutes in duration, all academic. They're held in insulated shacks, outbuildings, the lower levels of dormitories and houses, the dining hall now divvied up into three separate spaces. But the coziest classroom of all is reserved for upper level English classes—Natalie's living room with its parquet flooring and deep red built-in couches.

What courses do you choose of your own free will? Is the registration table spread with in-depth studies of J. D. Salinger or Mario Puzo? How about an exploration of sanity and madness, or the history of rock 'n' roll? Memoirs from drug addicts or convicts? Do you attend workshops about *feelings*, with Hermann Hesse's *Siddhartha* the only text? Is math off the table completely if students should so choose?

You wish. Both the American and Swiss programs follow a set of requirements that mirror those in public schools: English I, II, III; Algebra I, II, Trigonometry; Biology, Chemistry, and Physics; and so forth. Some are standard in content, as they have to be. Others are organized around themes, like "power" or "aesthetics" or "love." You, along with other students, are steered with little tugs on your shirtsleeves into small groupings of blended grade levels. In English, eleventh graders sit alongside twelfth graders. Twelfth graders grimace or fidget when tenth graders are struck dumb with intimidation.

Occasionally, science and math mix Swiss students and Americans who should be comfortable speaking German by now. With a maximum of twelve students in each course and sometimes far fewer, you *will* be found out if you've botched the homework or cannot recall the difference between *sinus und cosinus*. Herr Kohl's *Physik* class on the lower level of Osthaus holds a half dozen Swiss boys and you. Kohl is over six feet, handsome, socially awkward, and perhaps not the best of teachers. One morning he raises his wooden yardstick in the air, places it on a table, and randomly spins rather than call on a specific student to solve the first problem. Its inevitable arc wobbles, drags, slowly, slowly circling round to you, who has to break down a complex equation for the benefit of other students, in *German*, your grasp of the language just nine months along. You stand stock-still at the blackboard, head down, chalk quivering between your fingers till Kohl relieves you of your misery with a prickly, "*Bitte, setz dich.*" Please, go sit down.

For the motivated student, there's plenty of encouragement to follow a particular interest, such as preparation for the baccalaureate, or a fourth language—independent study Spanish with Linnea, or Esperanto, taught by that horsey fellow Gerard Cool, or all of Shakespeare's histories. For Americans, there's college prep, especially the obligatory SAT and Barron's formidable lists of vocabulary words. Plan on a full semester memorizing three hundred words a week, followed by pop quizzes. You will find only two such words appearing on the actual test, and they are from the end of the alphabet, by which time anyone's memory would be full up—*R* for *recidivism* and *T* for *tergiversate*. No room for those definitions in your little lunchbox of a brain.

One five-week period, you are turned loose on Dickens and read five fat novels, starting with *Our Mutual Friend*. It is transformative, sinking into another century thick with texture and pathos, just the cure for an anxious, self-absorbed teenager. The novels overwhelm you. They spill and spin, superimpose on your surroundings like holograms, bigger, wider, more real than the very real mountains and valleys. You half expect to see rats skitter over the tile or the little waif Johnny Higden curl up next to you in bed. "With a weary and yet a pleased smile, and with an action as if he stretched his little figure out to rest, the child heaved his body on the sustaining arm, and seeking Rokesmith's face with his lips, said: 'A kiss for the boofer lady.'" Your friends wonder where you've gone. When will you come back? But after finishing each book, you are terrible company, frantic to get it all down in your notebook and start the next novel.

Lunch, the main meal of the day, opens with soup concocted from yesterday's dinner. If served crepes on Tuesday, Wednesday those leftovers are sliced into long, speckled strips and now float in a salty brown broth. Thursday dinner featured polenta fried with onions and garlic; thus Friday the very same cornmeal is dissolved into tomato stock, or perhaps shaped and refried into little pancakes. The main course always contains potatoes, accompanied by green beans, cabbage, and occasionally *Lauch*, or boiled leeks. Dessert is virtually unheard of. Nor can you expect much meat, except on Sundays, when platters appear of foil-wrapped cheeses, pickles, butter, and *Cervelat* (sausages rather like plump hot dogs), two for each table. The village bakery sends up a tasty white sourdough with its crisp crust, and there is, praise God, chocolate for dessert, the bars split into uniform chunks and distributed by *Familie Eltern*.

But watch out. K.C. is a carnivore and waits all week for any sign of meat. One day (a *week*day!), two large, hot-to-the-touch plates appear with strips of some kind of flesh laid artfully across rice then doused in an aromatic brown sauce. He helps himself to a large portion, *piles* it on, and immediately begins shoveling it into his mouth. It is liver. He gags. What to do now? *Ach*, he is in the Lüthi family and today Armin sits directly across from him. Armin, with his rules and his strong opinions about American eating habits: They have such terrible attitudes toward food! They are so picky. He insists students eat everything, right down to that last sliver of carrot. "There is no bad food, there is only insufficient garlic," he trills. K.C. waits till Armin turns away and in a flash swaps his full plate with the empty one at the unoccupied seat beside him. For better effect, he scoops over a smidgeon of rice and sauce too. Armin is none the wiser.

When the dishes are empty, hopeful students thrust them into the air for a refill, but on Sundays, Service ignores them. Other days, there are seconds and thirds and fourths of anything you wouldn't want. A full menu follows.

brussel sprouts and mashed potatoes
lentil soup and servilla
lauch and fried potatoes
beans and french fries.
weise bohnen and boiled potatoes
fleisch kaese,sauerkraut and bioled potatoes
rattatooi and boiled potatoes
cauliflauer9blumenkohl) and fried potatoes
fish and tarter sause and boiled potatoes
fried eggs,that creamed spinach and bioled potatoes
once in a life time winerschnitzel.
italienische salat
reis salat
bauern hoernli
polenta
boildd potatoes and sour cream
muesli,quark and haferflocken
roeschti
spagetti
rice and the left over spagettia sauce
potatoes in brown sauce
cassarole with potatoes and tomatoes
rice and peas
Cold Cuts on Paulus's birthday
cheering Hiya,hyia hiya,with David Matson looking li
a fool doing it!
Sundays and the special cold plate,with Gala cheeze,
yellow cheeze,pickles,sardines,tomatoes,liverwurst,
and sometimes yogurt.
Breakfa st are always the same-brown bread and white
bread with butter and confi,and kakao,and porrige.
Sudays with mollases
Apples,then soup,then potatoes and beans,and maybe
dessert.and then mail!

Menu items and other Speisesaal details.

Mittagsrühe (obligatory), or afternoon quiet. With a belly full of starches, you welcome a nap, so take the short cut that runs behind the kitchen and smells like onions and guarantees you'll sink into your pillow just a little earlier than if you loped along the road with its more gradual pitch and lone cow tied to a fence. Or maybe you're feeling productive. Cut up some flash cards for tomorrow's hundred-word vocab test, and then read the last act of *The Winter's Tale*. Or type letters home on your baby Olivetti and thin blue stationery stamped *Mit Luftpost* or *Par Avion*. A stamp costs five centimes but you can also buy postage, paper, and envelope in one all-inclusive piece, then seal the edges with a lick.

How this featherweight little nothing makes it all the way from isolated Goldern to big city Washington, D.C., is nothing short of astonishing.

And how might a parent react to that throwaway sentence—"I got drunk again a few nights ago, it was so much fun"—buried at the bottom of this letter, a possibly dangerous but most definitely *serious* Ecole infraction. Would it be wise to send a telegram? Alert the directors? Create of storm of negativity in her precarious adjustment overseas? Unglue the trust the girl has for her mom? You can only imagine.

In the tamped-down atmosphere of rest hour, your inner squirrel begins to settle. Climb up onto your desktop, sit cross-legged before the picture window, and take in the mountains, plush indigo in afternoon light. It's not unproductive. Call it yoga or meditation, just becoming popular among westerners. Your eye follows the undulating tree line across the valley, interrupted by a cleft ripped by mudslide and avalanche. Then over the valley to the foreground, a small parking lot where a boy dressed in a down jacket pokes at a circle of ice with his boot tip. He taps lightly, withdraws, inches out again. So he's discovered it too, the many variations of frozen water, even here in an array of overlooked puddles. There are wafer-thin layers called cat's eyes that crackle at the slightest touch. There are ice bubbles like miniature lightbulbs that require a little more pressure. Finally, the solid

Dear Mom,
Sorry that my letter writing   not been   as it should
be but I just dno't have any time anymore. All the advertised
free time is wasted on such trivial things like plane movies
which teach me nothing. I8m finally reading a little bit (the
first book that hasn't been assigned since I got here) - Man
child in the Promise Land- that is the most fantastic book-
I just can't put it down. John my german teacher told me that
he thought I wasn't working up to my capacity and I guess I
agree but I just hadn't noticed how lazy I was getting so now
I will try extra hard. Math is so frustrating, of was, because
the whole class is behind and those who are ahead are not allow
ed to go on we have to wait #/#. Not only that but he refuses to
explain anything and assumes that we all know everything,(he
being he math teacher) that my dear is lazyiness. French is
really neat, we are writing all these compositions and I'm
seeing how weak my grammar. Well enough of the daily report.
It ahs snowed for three days straight and on and off for two
weeks,so in /other words,we have had no sunshine and four feet
of sn w here and about six feet up at Kaserstadt. I went skiing
two more times up there and each time was really beautiful
even though I was tired I did not get scared. Shakespeare is
wild and everyone forgets thier lines just when I don't happen
to be following the part so I make a fool of myself. I can't
wait till the reall thing. I have been having these rather
disturbing dreams about you,like I dreamt I was shot in the ba
ck and that you had to watch and I didn't care whether I was
dead but I really didn't want to see you hurt. oder? I got
drunk again a few nights ago,it was so much fun. Oh by the
way,they took my asperin away ahd told me to go to the nurse
if I got a headache, I did and she told me to go out in the fre
sh air. That didn't make me feel any better cause   as
Furn out. I miss every body very much.

                    Love,
                    Sarah

Letter to Mom 1.

stuff—nilas, frazil—that he jumps on and smashes to bits before running away. This is his modest collaboration with nature, and yours too, which you describe in a first-person paragraph for an English assignment. Your classmates love it and Richard agrees. Using your writing as springboard, he talks about detail versus abstraction and nearly everyone gets it.

▲▲▲ 3:15 p.m.

Cocoa and plain brown bread and sometimes apples are laid out in the dining room hall for anyone who desires a snack, but there are only a few takers.

▲▲▲ 3:30 to 5:30 p.m.

Afternoon courses are an integral part of each student's individual program. Students choose from an extensive array of music, sport, arts, and practical courses—courses which feed off of the creativity, inclinations, and professionalism of the teachers, and which offer students the opportunity to explore their talents and to discover unknown abilities in themselves.

Fraulein Pederson, also known as Pidi, hosts a leather class around her heavily scarred oak worktable in Gartenhaus. She heaps to one side embossing tools, hammers, punches, awls, and needles; empties on the other a bag full of scraps: suede, pig- and calfskin, chamois, fake, embossed, and polished. She delivers few instructions but pulls out a finished saddlebag and points to the tools she used. No single piece of leather will make a bag that large, so she plucks a bunch of triangles, squares, and strips to demonstrate how patchwork is more creative anyway. Few of her students share her gift. They should be wearing gloves. They drive needles into the table and burn blisters into their thumbs. You make a pencil pouch lacking a fastener, but it will be well used and ink stained anyway.

Or perhaps you'd like to study the natural flora of alpine pastures? Frau Varga might persuade you to build a dried, mounted herbarium

Pencil pouch, constructed in Pidi's leather workshop.

in addition to merely identifying each species. And she'll warn you that color drains from the bright blue gentian during this process, so don't be surprised if your specimen turns white.

You linger over the flower while it is still rooted in soil. This blue, this bit of cobalt trumpeting to the sky, is what you want to remember. So you fashion a kind of mental herbarium as well and pay little attention to the actual flower once it is plucked, mounted, and shuffled along in time.

Blue gentians.

Or, sign up for chorus, led by Herr Lüthi. It may take some courage; he's an intimidating figure and he's the school *Direktor*. But this is an opportunity to work with him on something you both love. The first piece is "Innsbruck ich muss dich lassen," by Heinrich Isaac (1450–1517). J. S. Bach picked up the song for one of his cantatas. It's that lovely. Here's the first verse:

> *Innsbruck, ich muss dich lassen,*
> *ich fahr dahin mein Strassen,*
> *in fremde Land dahin.*
> *Mein Freud ist mir genommen,*
> *die ich nit weiss bekommen,*
> *wo ich im Elend bin.*

A courtier has been fired, must leave the court and his beloved city. The music is melancholy and beautifully harmonized. Armin breaks down the bass, tenor, alto, and soprano and directs them individually, two run-throughs each, though there is only one tenor and his voice is rather tentative. Armin moves an alto over to help, but you can tell she's not happy singing with the boys. Then he slowly puts the music back together, line by line. The last bit is difficult, with a long flurry of notes around the word "Elend" that must be followed on the mark by all four voices. It's slow going and frustrating. He turns around briefly to regain his composure, then faces the group once more, slipping two fingers around his front tooth, which he suddenly extracts and raises into the air for everyone to see. It's *fake*! And there's a scary little spike at the base, which anchors it somewhere. A moment of stunned silence. Finally the choir detonates—HAHAHAHAHA! And practice continues on a lighter note. No wonder he refers to himself as "the palace fool," taskmaster with a malleable face and a strange sense of humor.

    ▲▲▲ 6:30 p.m.

The dinner bell sounds and by now you're famished. But the evening means light eating to the Swiss: a little leftover soup and bread or a helping of *Birchermüsli* or *Birchermuesli*, a practical one-pot meal of finely chopped walnuts, fresh apple, sunflower seeds, raisins, wheat bran, wheat germ, and rolled oats. The word *Muesli* stems from *Mues*, which is related to the Old English *moose*, meaning stew or pottage. Alas, you with your high metabolism will be hungry again by bedtime unless for snacking you've stored extra bowls of the stuff outside on your windowsill. In the winter, a crust of ice forms in just a couple of hours. In the spring or fall, the stuff is borderline digestible. Otherwise, count on *Fresspaketen* shipped overseas by your parents, if you are lucky.

Fressen translates "eat like an animal," and when these packages arrive you gorge on little boxes of Frosted Flakes or Cocoa Puffs, cinnamon graham crackers, Cup-a-Soup, SweeTARTS, beef jerky, Lik-M-Aid, and value bags of red licorice. Once, as a joke, your sister packs up a huge helping of turkey and mashed potatoes in a cigar box and sends it *by boat* for your first Thanksgiving away from home. You have no idea what she meant by the little heap of black dust you find staining the tissue paper six weeks later. Luckily there is a note.

Unless you have the gift of sharing, or the package is stolen, Fresspaketen can assuage both hunger and homesickness for a good while.

   ▲▲▲ 7:30 to 8:00 p.m.

Singgemeinde (obligatory), or "community sing," what you might call a sing-along. In the auditorium, a profusion of chairs are set in shrinking semicircles around taskmaster Herr Lüthi and his violin. The kids tumble in and choose their seats, save others for their friends, or move, bringing the whole gang along. Armin raises a finger, and a long *shshshshsh* issues from teachers scattered about. With a quick cock of his chin, he reprimands the boy who throws his arm around his girlfriend and nuzzles her neck, both of them blinking in embarrassment. Or the sleeper, dinner sinking in his stomach, now suddenly awake: "William, perhaps you would like to sing this alone?" There's irony and humor in his voice, an effective light touch.

"Today, my friends, we'll concentrate on *rounds*." How ingenious to adopt this musical form. It's so teachable. One hundred thirty-five students, many of them adolescents, broken into three sections: left, center, right. First the entire room executes the round in unison. Then, each section separately. Finally alternate entrances—left, center, right—till they create a cascade of notes, lyrics, harmony, echoes, and rhythmic counterpoint. It is a gorgeous sound. If you believe teenagers love only their music, their rock 'n' roll and Motown, then listen to this: a saucy Purcell, an ancient Israeli dirge, a French love song, performed by a bunch of scruffy kids who, by force and perhaps a little desire, abandon their interest in anything else.

Besides, Armin's got his eye on you and always knows when someone's not singing.

▲▲▲ 8:00 p.m.

Freizeit. Time for walks and electric guitars without the amps. Time for flirting and cruel teasing and lighting farts with matches. Time for trading shirts and braiding lanyards and Risk. Practice the European method of knitting, which frees the gaze, then knit a maroon sweater and simultaneously read all of *The Godfather*, neither requiring all that much concentration. Time for delivering love notes and expecting too much. Time for hovering outside doors pretending to smoke with a blade of straw. Time for pranks and show-offs risking splinters by sliding down banisters on their butts. Free time to impress, to gather news and gossip, to figure out whether it's you they meant to insult or flatter. Time for you and your new friend K.C. to share stories about girlfriends and boyfriends and how far you got with each. You're aiming for home plate. He had to leave his sweetheart back in D.C. No question, you're testing the romantic waters between you. Lukewarm? Too hot? Don't think so. A bell rings, the gong circles, and now it is time for bed. Good-bye tiniest freedom, sudden flight of precious minutes.

▲▲▲ 9:00 p.m.

Lights out.

Your body elongates like elastic but breakable, distressed by things small and irritating. Dry skin around the nose, goose down pricking your shoulder. Nothing compared to the frenetic thinking, made worse by the fear of frenetic thinking. You can't get to sleep. Your roommate is already snoring. Ice-coated branches clack against the window. You're solving an endless mathematical problem that should be easy, like eight times four. But the eights leap away before you can count them. To slow your heart, you imagine walking home, the many miles of small footsteps, tedious small footsteps, like those of sheep swapping fields, but counting sheep never works for you. They make too much noise; they bump against a sign anchored in the soil reading: *I cannot fall asleep.* A yardstick of moonlight squeezes through the window. This means your eyes are open. You can't even shut your eyes, the only person in Goldern who isn't sleeping.

When desperate, swallow a half tablet of Nembutal without water, very bitter. A last resort, since the doctor warned they are addicting and he rarely prescribes more than a dozen. Reserve three for the three nights before the SATS, so that leaves seven. Soon the body begins to melt, shoulder blades to big toe. It's like stepping into a bath. Muscle and bone dissolve, cold slithers into hot, and everything slows down, down, down, down, down. . . .

Bites ⋀⋀ *Potatoes*

Kartoffeln kartoffeln, wir essen gern kartoffeln. (Potatoes potatoes, we love to eat potatoes.) Leave it to the Swiss to come up with a high-spirited cheer when meat is too expensive, fruit (except for apples) dreadful because trucked in from a million miles away, and the only vegetable impossible to forget is spinach because it is so unattractively served— creamed, sloshed on a platter topped with fried eggs (*Spinat und Spiegeleier*) and then only on Saturdays.

But potatoes! Boiled, parsleyed, draped with cheese, or sprinkled with scallions. The Swiss were slow to engage in plain old baked and why bother when they have *Rösti*—roughly grated, mixed with minced onion, fried in butter, where the crust turns a golden brown, then flipped onto a plate like a pancake, a divine hemisphere. German- and French-speaking areas of the country each claim Rösti as their own invention and oh, they are serious. Between them lies the battleground; there's even a name for it—the *Röstigraben* or Rösti ditch.

Potatoes flicker and glow, like mother in our bellies. Home (oh yes) is where the potatoes are.

The Twin Cities ⟋⟍⟍ *Heimweh*

When the neurotic complains that the world
does not understand him, he is telling us in a word
that he wants his mother.
—CARL JUNG

The community is organized into pedagogical "families," and much of its uniqueness stems from the fact that the teachers are at the same time "family heads." The constant presence and accessibility of adults who assume such diverse roles accentuates a sense of solidarity and common purpose, and leads to trusting relationships between teachers and students. Both community life and academic pursuits profit from these close relationships.

▲▲▲

Here commences the fusion of pedagogy and childrearing typical of *Landerziehungsheimen*. Four to twelve students, equal numbers of boys and girls from a variety of cultures, all living together in a house located directly on or close to campus. The teachers may be married with children of their own and those children too will be raised as Ecolianers. There are family evenings, family hikes, family meals. The idea is to create an intimate homelike atmosphere far away from home.

My first set of ersatz parents was the Swiss family Rohrer from Basel. From the start I associated Hanspeter with "saltpeter" and never could break off the picture of encrusted rock as his big forehead moved in and out of my field of vision. His boots were systematically laced and planted deliberately, up and down like hydraulic hammers. His shirts, even the flannel ones, were crisp, tucked in to high-waist khakis though everyone else in the world let their flaps hang out. He tried hard to work a balance of warmth and discipline, with that neat goatee and forced laugh, but when willing a genial gesture, he seemed even scarier, tense and phony. I was ever ready for the first impatient jab as he watched over our breakfast clean up and bed making. "Try it this way. No, not quite." His wife, Magdalene, was hugely pregnant, sweet and pale as honeydew. She appeared to be afflicted with something I could only sense: a dangerous naïveté, chronic lung disease? She rarely smiled and kept to herself in their overheated apartment. We could have used her female influence but she hardly looked older than we were. I remember thinking: *Surely she will die young.* Cell phones did not exist—should I have hung a sheet from the window to alert a social worker, if one happened by?

These were my *in loco parentum*, further from my own parents than the earth from Mars. They could have *been* Martians, landing in the spacecraft-like dormitory Osthaus, freshly constructed of durable but echoing tile and cement. This too was a long way from my built-in-1862 childhood home in D.C. with its worn-down wooden floors and wobbly newel posts. I suspect my parents felt guilty about shipping me off but more than once my mother remarked how quiet the house was with "only" four girls around. She wrote often, on Clark stationery with address engraved in blue (1561 Thirty-Fifth Street, Washington 7, D.C.), and steadfastly assured I was missed and much beloved.

And yet, and yet. . . . My sisters have moved into the space I used to occupy. They wear my cast-off necklaces and blossom in the unimpeded attention of my parents. Nancy is now the eldest (always the most mature) and reads her entire research paper aloud at the dining room table. Dad listens close enough to suggest she beef up the conclusion. Jenny sits down at the upright piano and plays Bach's Prelude in C with an ease and imagination I never quite mastered. Does she feel me circling, a ghost wolf, anxious to tear her down? Do they slip into my third-floor bedroom and steal or desecrate the small objects I left behind? Kim lifts just four pink-foam curlers, enough to flip the ends of her very straight hair, but not enough to register the theft. Jenny borrows my enamels and paints herself a messy box. She's careful to screw the lids back on so they don't dry up, ever wary of my thunder.

I want to tell them: This is *my* Switzerland. Better than your Georgetown. Better than P Street beach and the park on Q and all your Unitarian friends. Look at my *international* friends: Anka, Barbara, Francesca, Sonia, Ulrike, and Helle, who, like me, have learned to stem Christie. I have a *passion* for potatoes and Gruyère cheese. Look at me working the Swiss franc and lowly rappen, hiking the steep trail up to the gondola and never complaining. I have adapted easily and have grown to appreciate the schedule. No such schedule at home!

Truthfully my sisters are glad *not* to see me every day and sometimes they even invite friends over to sleep in my bedroom. When my mother whispers to herself, "If I could just close my eyes for five minutes," they let her. My sisters play with her hair, and she leans back with a slow, blissful sigh.

I fashioned an eight-by-eleven calendar and hung it under the top bunk next to my pillow. Three months till winter break, each day a square, obliterated with a large red X. Three months of following the path up to Osthaus and down again, sitting through my classes, eating my polenta, practicing my vocabulary words. Anka is waving a bar of chocolate in my face. But I'm not here and she seems stupidly Swiss. I'm four thousand miles west. It hurts to be in a beautiful place, even if it's a gift—a guaranteed "good experience"—and to feel that you're the oddball or maybe the only sane one surrounded by a bunch of oddballs.

Decades later, landlocked in America pining four thousand miles east for my Switzerland, I had a Sebaldian moment: The past, distant in years, character, and geography, rises up to match the present, *my* present. Not a perfect match of course, but similar enough to jolt as when you are reading a novel in which a train *jounces* through nineteenth-century Eastern Europe and at that moment a passerby utters the very same word, *jounces*. These small coincidences suggest a fine network of points and connecting arrows, similarities traveling through four dimensions, across time and space to assure us that no flower, thought, blood type, wind, wrinkle or fold of skin, grass, or dilemma is ever truly singular: The Swiss invented the word for homesickness. Of course they did!

A medical scholar named Johannes Hofer was thinking of me four centuries ago in 1688 when he observed the following symptoms in a patient—sadness, a longing for the Alps, and "burning fever." The patient was living in Basel, just sixty miles from his home in Bern, but it might as well have been four thousand miles, for daily his physical and emotional state worsened till it appeared the man would surely expire. A decision was made to return him to his native city so he could die in peace surrounded by family. Thus his bed was loaded onto a wagon and transported to Bern. The journey took time, days in fact, and as each hour passed, he began to breathe easier, speak freely with his fellow travelers, until "all the symptoms abated to such a great extent they really relaxed altogether, and he was restored to his whole sane self."

Hofer was aware of the French expression *la maladie du pays* and the German *Heimweh*, later known as *Schweizerheimweh*, since the condition appeared in numerous homesick mountain-loving Swiss soldiers stationed in Italy and France. Other symptoms included dizziness, nausea, and lack of appetite. Some military doctors blamed early exposure to incessant, ear-splitting cowbell clanging, which resulted in loss of balance and brain damage.

But, according to Hofer, no one had thus far summed up nor accurately described both the medical symptoms and devastating emotions of Heimweh, a "neurological disease of essentially demonic cause." Thus he felt obliged to come up with a new word in his Basel dissertation—the fancier term "nostalgia," from the Greek νόστος ἄλγος (*nostos* and *algos*), meaning "homecoming," and "pain, ache." Along with the medical view of nostalgia came notions of disease management and possible cures. Doctors turned to opiates, lukewarm emulsions, stomach and intestinal flushes, leeches, and as a last resort, a return to the Alps.

I do not think I suffered from nostalgia as it has come to mean: a longing for a certain *time* that no longer exists. Nor was I yearning for *place*: my family house built of stone situated at the corner of Thirty-Fifth and Q.

No, I missed my mother. Therefore the inevitable but unfair comparison between Magdalene Rohrer and Peggy Gorham. Thus the hoarding of Mom's letters, which I sniffed for evidence of her mother-smell, that mixture of soap and mildewed sponge. Sprinkled here or there, a tiny nonpareil of coffee no more alive than a thumbtack. In my melancholic mind I drew up the cup myself—thick handled restaurant type with a light lipstick stain. Was it her eighth or ninth cup? Was it past ten, everyone in bed but my mother? No, my father was traveling. New York, California, Omaha. I saw her rolling onionskin into her Royal typewriter, keys clip-clopping away. Paper yanked out—another smudge, rubbed with her thumb—as she thought about what else to pop into the envelope, maybe a *Peanuts* cartoon, and here I couldn't help feel a tinge of disappointment as it referred not to me, but to my sister Jenny, nicknamed Heff.

Finally, the licked stamp, her tongue coffee scented, not yet old-person-unbearable, though she tested all her girls with a saliva-soaked thumb rubbed across our dirty mouths, even as teenagers.

My imagination was deft but ultimately inadequate. I slipped between the flowered sheets she bought me at Hecht's department store and sunk into the goose down pillow she loaned me from her own bed. These things were temporarily mother herself, but like all objects from a distant beloved, they teetered between consoling and biting. So *chilled*, till I warmed and loosened them up myself, myself, myself.

God forbid I reveal any lip quiver or all-out wallowing. All around me were students young and old who carried on as if it were perfectly reasonable to be living in a miniscule, isolated community in exile from their real families. Seven-year-old Jeannette, with her long blond locks, who accidently swallowed an open safety pin and was rushed to the hospital in Lucerne, where they observed her till it passed through her system. All without her mother. Ten-year-old Tommy, who traipsed up and down the stairs dragging a large stick against the balusters. He was no wimp. Even today, many of the American faculty consider themselves ex-pats and, at least on the surface, do not miss their homes beyond the Alps and over the great Atlantic Ocean. Every cultural clue in my new surroundings deflected the possibility I might miss my mother.

Friday

Dearest Sah,

I'm procrastinating. I hate the thought of returning to the mess my final report is in. When this is over I am turning over a new leaf! No more drudgery!

Enclosed is a peanuts cartoon that fits Heff to a T.

Haven't had a letter from Dad yet. I know he's having a great time though. He's just the kind of person that gets an enormous amount out of travel. I wish I were with him.

Today I am to try to get Benjy out of her English class. She cannot stand her English teacher.

I do hope you won't have any more bad dreams. Are you all right? Do remember that if you stop being happy there, come home! But I assume still that you are in the very best of all possible places for you and that what is happening now to your emotions is really a working out of old problems. They are surfacing where you can confront them, and that's good.

Anyhow, I love you and can't wait til the 19th. It's going to be so great!

Mom

Letter from Mom.

Homesickness was disabling—a murky, muddy no-man's-land that slowed your progress into the community and above all served no practical purpose. When a teenager wanted to be an adult more than anything else in the world, homesickness was a sign of immaturity, even infancy.

Throughout much of history, Heimweh evolved into something to suppress. Switzerland sent its mercenaries to Italy and France but also enacted a law forbidding them to sing cow-herding songs—*Kuhreihen*—for fear they would all fall weeping and set off immediately for their homeland. A diagnosis of nostalgia was thought to be an insult among soldiers elsewhere as well. American Civil War physician Theodore Calhoun considered it unmanly. He and other doctors believed the disease contained a immoral component, leading to daydreaming, indolence, and excessive sexual desire. You don't want to be the one who set out in search of adventure only to encounter dislocation and immutability. You certainly didn't want this to get in the way of work.

Weeks into the trimester, I resolved to live in another family in a much older dorm. No adjusting to the Rohrers and their alien physiognomy. To my relief there was a policy that allowed just that: Think carefully about what family suits you, talk it over, put in your request to *Konferenz*, and the school will try to accommodate you.

Lucky K.C., who had no appalling first experience like the Rohrers. He chose the Lüthis right off the bat, or the Lüthis chose him, it was never clear. He was most certainly a chosen boy—bright, hardworking, and well behaved. He made friends easily, loved sports and games of all kinds, and was unusually sensitive to how other people felt. Under Natalie and Armin's care, he quickly learned the Ecole ideals and principles. He became active in the student council (*Kameradenrat*), leader of the *Schulegemeinde* (community meeting), and was elected to the very first *Vertrauensrat* (peer counseling group). He set up the school's first recycling program and worked with friends to establish a school newspaper, *Die Reutikiste*. There were a handful of others like him, respected by their peers, steered toward a life of responsibility, teaching, even a directorship someday.

Me? I chose Pidi, or Fraulein Pederson, another kind of extraterrestrial, but this one came endorsed by friends because her oversight was lax. She rested on the adorable end of the peculiar spectrum. Native German, she made little attempt to learn English or any other language, even *Schweizerdeutsch*. Hard of hearing, then years later totally deaf, this half-listening drove her personality, for she did what she pleased, where, and when. Everyone wanted to be in her family. But I got a tip from Barbara, who ended up as my roommate: "Give her a kiss. Pick any opportunity. She won't hear you anyway and God knows what she'll be thinking." A few days before the Konferenz when Familie requests were being considered, Pidi was on the *Sportplatz* instructing a crew of sweepers in the fine art of gravel control. I snuck up from behind and bussed her on the cheek. She startled. Her set, determined gaze broke, eyelids twittering. Around her upper lip were short vertical lines like coding above a mass mail address. As she smiled, they briefly disappeared. Pidi was honestly touched. I was in.

Thus began in earnest my assimilation into the community and transference from longed-for genetic mother to fun-loving replacement. Here's a typical Pidi entrance: knock once on a door with one hand and push with the other, simultaneously. No point in waiting for an inaudible response. There she stood in her work clothes and cropped hair, slight in frame, arms stringy with tendons and perpetually tan. No matter if she found us towel-wrapped or asleep in our underpants. No consequences if a boyfriend squirmed under the duvet or she interrupted a weepy conversation. Her face was an olive stood on end, with two black specks for eyes, and from it emerged a voice pinched and nasal, utterly flat unless she was pissed, which we rarely saw. She was there for practical reasons: to recruit Barbara for a German play, to announce a workshop in mosaics or new location for her woodworking class. In this eccentric approach, she was hard to resist; we felt compelled and a little sorry for her.

Pidi's family lived in the four-story Turmhaus, another attraction for many students because it was *the* social hub. Iconic tower with its bell. Catenary floorboards and rubbed-to-a-shine banisters that only occasionally gave off splinters. S-shaped door handles and loose locks,

Family head, Pidi, at dinner in the Speisesaal.

their hardware jiggling open with a light push. Scratchy army blankets and huge sacklike comforters, the down pooling at the bottom as you shook them out each morning. Third-story rooms with woodpeckers hammering above their ceilings and that smell of old timber and wet boots and melted snow. The big boys jumping into the drifts several stories below and walking away unharmed. My dangerous perch on the top balcony railing, legs tucked around a post, just to be sure.

At one point, the Ecole's insurer declared the worn-out building unfit for occupation but agreed to allow the school two more years to come up with the money for an alternate residence. Pidi took the place on. She would not have her students living in a dump so she spent her summers and three-week breaks fixing it up, repairing banisters, sanding stairs, hanging paintings, and landscaping. This was no singular occurrence. She took on some of the sorriest, most disturbed students the same way: lots of one-on-one tutoring and made-to-order challenges.

Pidi herself lived in a small, weather-beaten cottage called Gartenhaus, directly behind Turmhaus. I saw it just once. The floors were layered with dusty Tunisian throw rugs in reds, yellows, and royal blues. There were enormous, sagging cushions instead of chairs. Her art was tacked to the walls wherever there was room, lovely wispy watercolors and pencil sketches. A tea station sat under a window frame and various Knorr soups, biscuits, and herbs burst out of a low shelf. The bed too was on the floor and I loved her even more now that I knew where she lived.

Her Familie hikes were notorious. Traipsing through the Italian hills on rocky footing, no hostels in sight, she invited herself and a dozen exhausted students into a farmer's barn for the night. The owner was generous. Around dinnertime, his sons appeared outside our glowing campfire with bottles of homemade wine. Everyone drank, "So as not to offend," said Pidi. Later, in the barn filled with freshly mown hay, half of the group was violently ill; vomit sunk into the bales or stained pajamas and sleeping bags. Her story to Konferenz blamed the hay—stored too early, too wet, moldy even. Were her colleagues aware such a thing might even cause spontaneous combustion? Her colleagues should consider *that*. Many raised eyebrows and mouths agape among the teachers crowded around the table, but not for the reasons she intended.

Pidi went solo in leading her family. No other teacher could or would share the responsibility. Students revered her, but the staff had their issues. To some she was dangerous, at best marginal—a crazy old woman with wiry hair who might have been gay and who sometimes wore white suits.

▲▲▲

Where is *home*? A birthplace? Or must we have been raised there? What about ancestors, so many of them immigrants? Do they still call Germany, Sweden, Portugal, Turkey, Japan, Wales, or England home?

Is a genetic inheritance enough to claim a long-ago country as our home too? Certainly a mother existed who made sure her children chewed their nettles and laced up their leather high-tops, who also sat at a small table in a corner, writing letters on onionskin to her loved ones in villages not so far away. Is the line connecting that hardworking mother of six to my hardworking mother of five so very diluted as to be entirely dissimilar?

Heimatort is the Swiss term that addresses these questions all at once. Also known as *Bürgerort*, it's where your family originated, the home you inherited from your father, his father before that, and all the way back. Stemming from the German *Heimat*, it nestles together descendance, community, and tradition—all elements of a person's identity. "Mother" virtually disappears from the equation. In Switzerland, women had no right to a Heimatort until 1988, when marital law was adopted. Before that, a wife had to adopt both her husband's name *and* place of origin.

The concept arose during Europe's industrial revolution, when the countryside lost many of its inhabitants to urban areas. It served to link populations to their previous, more intimate communities, while reinforcing their individuality. Heimatort brought together dialect, family, and place in a tidy package. The word is today stamped on every Swiss passport, under a heading translated into two other primary Swiss languages: "*lieu d'origine*" and "*luogo di attinenza*," with the English "place of origin" thrown in as well. This, though you may have been born elsewhere, though generations may have passed since anyone in your family actually lived there.

The little village of Goldern in Hasliberg is home and Heimatort to the Familie Hirsig, as well as several other families who have lived here for generations—Neiger, Schild, Huggler. Until not so long ago, thanks to the benefits of Heimatort, these folks were entitled to a share of the milk and cheese produced in the mountain pastures above. They could also graze their cow or goat in a community meadow and stake claim to some of the wood cut down from forests in the area. If they ventured into the city of Basel or Zurich and lost their financial footing, then the Hasliberg had to take care of them.

Today, for practical reasons, these benefits have begun to fade. Why should a community like Goldern provide social services for a struggling mother of three (born in Geneva, living in Lausanne, America, or England) whose descendants haven't lived in the Hasliberg for four or five generations? The concept has morphed into quaint tradition, though the Swiss are still serious about place of origin. Driving through the Haslital, one quickly discovers that even road names are rooted in and loyal to their various territories. In Meiringen, Liechtenenstrasse becomes Hauptstrasse, then Bahnhofstrasse, which morphs into Alpbachstrasse, all within a kilometer or two.

The Hirsigs run the Hotel Gletscherblick, an old-fashioned hotel that has changed little since its construction more than a hundred years ago. It would serve very well as Nabokov's or any famous writer's home, except that this establishment, unlike the Montreux Palace on Lake Geneva, is quite modest. Facing east, there's a magnificent view of the Wetterhorn cluster through large windows on each of five levels. There are fewer windows on the other side, but that's the way houses are built here—into the hillside to insulate against the cold. A two-person elevator hisses up and down from roof terrace to dining room and lounge, which lie on either the main floor or three floors up, depending on where you enter the building. It takes some getting used to.

Elise Hirsig and her husband Gottlieb opened the Gletscherblick in 1907. A collage of photos hangs next to the lift beginning with Elise (1867–1967) and Gottlieb (1873–1922) and ending with their five grandchildren: Johannes (1945), Annelies (1946), Rosine (1947), Christine (1949), and Peter (1960). Christine is the only child dressed in an apron, required for school. Actually, she tells me, it's a half-apron, a privilege granted to girls above the age of ten. The young ones wear a full.

Christine, Peter, and his wife, Fiona, ran the place for a number of years, but Christine is the one you see the most, ever present though she claims to take an evening off in Brienz, where she has herself a nice meal near the sea. The Hirsigs have been here so long—"all my life," she says—they know precisely how to care for the guests: how to make a sauce or a salad dressing or how to set a tray of silver-plated pitchers for breakfast, one hot water, one steamed milk, and one coffee, dark with a foam scrim. A buffet is laid out under a "Peter Sneezegaard," as one visitor jokes, the only sign of change and new government requirements. Baskets of local bread; farm cheeses, all sliced and ready to lift with a fork onto your plate; meats; boiled eggs, their shells dyed a swirl of orange and yellow; muesli; corn flakes; as well as little aluminum packets of jam, honey, Nutella, and butter. The milk is rich. The butter is true. The paper napkins are folded and propped up on the table like pup tents. Lunchtime, the buffet is loaded with meat and gravy, boiled vegetables, and parsleyed potatoes. Workers wearing neon shin guards come in from a village construction site, where they are expanding the local school, scraping off the concrete playground and swinging two-by-fours about. There is no sign of pressboard, only solid wood, and it's a beautiful yellow pine.

Christine leans close to my ear and says in a very low voice, "I need to ask you a question."

I'm startled, expecting bad news.

"Tonight, rice or potatoes with your steak?"

She is trilingual, though thoroughly fluent only in her native Schweizerdeutsch. To each question or complaint she reacts with quiet concern. Impeccably sweet, she never raises her voice and instructs her staff with whispers. A slightly slope-backed figure (osteoporosis seems to run in the family) with soft white hair, large blue eyes, and comfortable clothes. An occasional moment of stress arrives with those downhill construction workers, who stir up the hallways and porches then leave like a receding tsunami. She sighs, "It is over." Little has changed here in forty-two years, except for a renovation initiated by the nieces that kept the heart of the hotel intact. Thus it feels like returning to family after a long absence. In fact, many guests give this hotel five *hearts*, since they "don't do stars here."

Forty-six years ago, I needed a little softness of the kind Pidi held back. On my sixteenth birthday, I pocketed my mother's gift of twenty Swiss francs and hiked up to the Gletscherblick to baste in the Hirsigs' calm attention. Christine was then a teenager herself, with half apron and straight brown hair pulled back into a small bun. Her parents must have been around, but Christine was the girl I remember, caring, it seemed, for only me:

> Here is a larger towel to lay out in the sauna [pronounced "sow-oo-na"]. Here a sample can of Nivea to restore your chapped skin. When the telephone will not cooperate, let me try. The number might be wrong. Let me check. Not a problem, I will dial. Let me speak to the airlines myself to arrange shipment of your lost suitcase. We feel sorry for you, one of those orphaned American students, stealing away from school to order ice cream in a silver champagne glass, served by someone kind, like me, who wears a half-apron like your mother's. You Americans are a rowdy bunch; you always leave a mess around the ice bath. But we like you. We serve you as if you were family.

There was something in her manner that worked like a sedative. I was transported four thousand miles home, my mother leaning over the rumpled bed where I lay on my stomach. Despite her own exhaustion, she sat down next to me, pushed my nightgown up to the shoulder blades, and ran her hands lightly up and down my back. My fingertips began to tingle and my mouth went slack, a blissful sensation that must be akin to a baby sloshing about in utero. When Christine with a polite nod of her head left me to sweat in the sauna or to savor my coffee ice cream, I often hung there, temporarily immobilized. Finally, my body recalibrated—for it had to—and I walked away on my own two feet.

Independence is what American culture demanded of me when a host of mothers fell under the influence of Dr. Spock. I could have been an infant, toddler, schoolgirl, or high school graduate about to head off to college—all counsel steered toward a healthy leave-taking from family. An infant sleeps successfully when alone, whether in a co-sleeper, a crib in the same room, or down the hall. If a toddler clings, it's called "separation anxiety" and parents are encouraged to take away the pacifier, the blanket she curls up in, the pillow she drags around the house. These are tokens of dependency and might delay her speech or interfere with her ability to walk. A "big girl" is one who does things for herself. She ties her own shoes, selects the clothes she will wear, and makes her own breakfast. She may even exhibit signs of "leadership" by helping her younger siblings in the morning. Shipping a daughter or son off to camp was a requisite ritual, whether the child wanted it or not. It's little wonder kids suffered, and still suffer, from diarrhea, acid reflux, and a host of other physical symptoms of Heimweh.

Away from home, I learn to accept various "tokens of dependence." This meant convincing myself that Pidi was a passable substitute for my mother and ignoring the fact that I paid for Christine's heavenly service and rejuvenating desserts. I accepted what consolation was out there, no matter the obvious deficiencies, as long as I didn't collapse under the weight of homesickness. I rode the little two-passenger elevator up to the third floor of Hotel Gletscherblick against school rules, paid with verboten pocket money, stripped down to my underwear, and entered the little sauna, with its teak platform. I threw a bit of water on the stones, stretched out on my worn towel as the enveloping heat slipped into my skin and lungs, urging my body to relax, loosen, weep.

The Not-So-Awful (Swiss) German Language

In 1878, Mark Twain toured southern and central Europe, a trip that resulted in his famous fiction/memoir hybrid *A Tramp Abroad*. It's one of three travel books and includes as appendix D the most hilarious essay ever written about a foreigner's struggle to learn a new tongue— "The Awful German Language." Even if it refers to the particularly overwrought German of the late nineteenth century, many of his complaints remain relevant:

- Too many rules and far too many exceptions to those rules.
- Too many novel-long words that "require the speaker to deliver them in sections, with intermissions for refreshments."
- Never-ending sentences that, with no reasonable explanation, split verbs in two and withhold half till the bitter end. Depending how long the sentence is, it's possible to forget there's an action word on its way. And imagine the United Nations translator who must thrum her fingers, waiting for the longed-for reunion of "was" and "born," then rush to catch up while dignitaries from other countries have moved on to another subject entirely. Why so complicated? Why not lasso that all-important verb from the hinterland and place it righteously up front, side-by-side with its subject?

Twain sums it up like this: "A gifted person ought to learn English (barring spelling and pronouncing) in thirty hours, French in thirty days, and German in thirty years. It seems manifest, then, that the latter tongue ought to be trimmed down and repaired."

Ach, but my blood is a kind of German stone soup: Homanns, Dunkelmeiers, Goldfarbs, Goldmans, and Goldbergs with a few

Russians and Poles for good measure, most of them poor, many of them peasants. I imagine them bobbing gently in swim caps and old-fashioned bathing suits, perhaps with a few root vegetables thrown in. My mother's people mixed with my father's people, Christian and Jew, intelligent and slow, solemnly stroking toward or away from each other depending on the current. When she cracked a dirty joke, my grandmother switched the punch line to Yiddish. My grandfather muttered, "*Ja, ja,*" when he didn't care to engage.

It's one reason why I took to the language, why I picked up conversational German in under three months at an international boarding school in Switzerland. I liked its exactitude. The *ch* sound, with tongue pressed against upper palate. *Tz* zipped through the right and left cuspids. And the wonderful rolling *r*s when a bit of fun and flourish was called for. Instead of Italian's romantic breezes and milkweed, German lets us speak in blades, diamond-sharp, flipped and whizzing through the air at supersonic speed. No fluff in sight.

I loved that nouns are capitalized—like a cheat sheet when forced to diagram a sentence. And once you mastered the alphabet, you could sound out any word, unlike the English nightmare of thought, laughter, night, and cough.

I collected what Twain disparaged. Big words were a sign of sophistication, grown-up talk. Here's an incredibly muscular Word of the Year named by the German Language Society: *Rindfleischetikettierungs-überwachungsaufgabenübertragungsgesetz,* or "Beef Labeling Supervision Delegation Act." That's sixty-three letters, no list of exceptions required for perfect pronunciation. It's so *determined,* so clear-cut in its authority, so intensely cadenced in a snare drum kind of way, making it the perfect soundtrack for musical chairs or chopping a sausage into bite-sized pieces. Yes sir. Right sir. You either comply or you don't and suffer the consequences.

And oh, I must disagree with Mr. Twain. Examine the exquisite *architecture* of German sentences where verbs were sliced up and shuffled about like Scrabble pieces. Not only could you place one section in the center and toss its mate to the end. You could also nestle other verbs nearby or squeeze in a verb-syllable or two to really stretch that thing out. The Swiss writer Friedrich Dürrenmatt wrote a novella (*The Assignment*) in twenty-four sentences, each chapter inspired by Bach's "Well-Tempered Clavier," each sentence running an average of 5.375 pages long before landing a single period. Those were some high-scoring sentences.

As for noun gender, I had to admit there was a problem. Forget English with its all-inclusive "the" and French, which limits gender to *le* and *la*, male and female. German employs male, female, *and* neuter. On top of that *der*, *die*, and *das* do not necessarily follow the obvious category of word, as in *das Mädchen*, dehumanizing a pretty girl by referring to her as "it." For example, this snippet of dialogue Twain translated from a German Sunday school book:

GRETCHEN: Wilhelm, where is the turnip?
WILHELM: She has gone to the kitchen.
GRETCHEN: Where is the accomplished and beautiful English maiden?
WILHELM: It has gone to the opera.

Before long, I had to face German Declension, wherein articles, adjectives, nouns, *and* pronouns themselves change form depending on not just their gender but also their number and position in the sentence, whether nominative, accusative, genitive, or dative, so that the word "regiment" can appear as *das Regiment*, *des Regiments*, or *die Regimenter*. Well, I basically gave up and resorted to mumbling like a mustachioed Australian. Dropped my chin as the article and noun came around and rushed to the end of the sentence with hope in my heart. Most German speakers forgive you the confusion, and the nice ones jump in to help.

My German teacher bought me a little vocab book, schoolgirl blue, designed to fit neatly in the back pocket of my jeans. And though I hated to pause in conversation, not wanting to appear stupid or weak, I referred to it whenever I could.

Note the use of all caps, hopeful bulbous print meant to convey a bigger me. Note the one word I illustrated, *der Säufer*. No room for pink elephants, though the exploded bubbles (or were they belches?) sufficed. After a night or two of verboten wine, I knew exactly how a

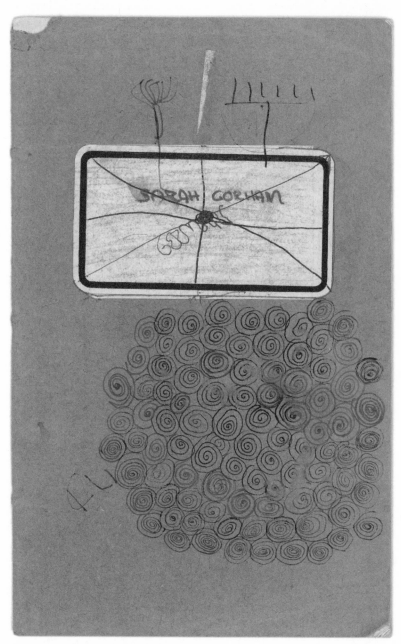

German vocabulary notebook, cover.

German vocabulary notebook, inside pages.

drunk felt. Note the words I would never need, or only as an adult, like *der Notar*, *die Taufe*, *der Witwer*. The vocabulary that stuck with me was specific to my age. Only later did I attempt the grown-up stuff.

Even then I made some awful mistakes. You'd think "That is my friend" would translate *Das ist mein Freund*, right? No, the German construction is more awkward: *Das ist ein Freund von mir* (That is a friend of mine). The former translates "That is my boyfriend," a socially slippery slope, depending on whom you are referring to. Alas, I was referring to Tobias Loosli, my first and most devastating crush. Oh, his adorable globe of a face, swept with bangs that roughly matched his windburned cheeks. Stocky is what we might call him now but on skis he floated, drawing a rippled line down the steepest slopes. He was from Ottikon, near Zurich, and his parents were marionetteers. How cool was that? As soon as he slid into my radar my body followed him like a caboose. Flirting with Tobias during the peak of an unusual heat wave I ripped off my jacket and swore, "*Scheisse, ich bin heiss!*" (Shit, I'm hot!) I could not imagine what he was laughing about, slapping his knees till they burned red. Someone finally whispered, did I really want to admit I was *that* horny?

No one can argue that German does not contain some of the coolest words and expressions in the world, virtually untranslatable into any other language. Beyond the well-known prince *der Weltschmerz* and princess *die Schadenfreude*, and even the slumming *Katzenjammer*, here are a few I adopted quickly and learned to love.

Keine Angst. No fear, my scaredy-cat. Strong but soothing as if your father were a war hero and stood by you in his olive-green uniform and maybe he is not alive and maybe he is, but if he isn't, you've internalized his reassurance, a tea light glowing inside your solar plexus.

Zimmer. Room. Pure and simple. In origins it mixes easily with *timber*, and most rooms I slept in were made of wood. But my primary association rests with Hans Zimmer, that ten year old with ice-blue eyes and shiny brown hair who socialized like a horsefly. Picture a bunch of tall guys around a hoop. Uninvited Hansi swoops in to grab the ball and refuses to give it back. Or he's a poor little *Waise* with no money from home, down on his knees begging for a bite of your chocolate bar. Go away Hans, *bitte*. Decades later it occurs to me: This is the same Hans Zimmer whose soundtrack for *The Lion King* wins an Oscar and *Gladiator* a Golden Globe. But little Hansi didn't last long, barely a year before he was shipped off to an even stricter boarding school in England. No one suspected he'd wind up among a handful of internationally famous alum.

Mach doch kein Theater. Quit playacting. Quit pretending the world has come to an end because Tobias is ignoring you. Maybe it feels that way, but catch a view from the outside. No one cares as much as you. My *God* how you care. Ridiculous. Get over yourself.

And, sandwiched inside that little phrase, the excellent *doch*. Emphatic, like *Er ist doch so blöd* (He is *so* stupid). Or *Das war doch Katarina* (That was *actually* Katarina). Versatile, used in various instances as "though," "after all," "however," "yet," "nevertheless," "why don't you," and trickiest of all, a kind of yes-no response rather like the French *si*, which doesn't exist in English. "So are you going or not?" *Doch doch* (Yes, yes, implying, "Of course I'm going"). Finally, someone might argue *Das stimmt nicht!* (That's not true!), provoking the response *Doch! Das stimmt!* (I beg to differ. It is true!).

Genau. Exactly. Smooth things out. Just what I was thinking. Spoken with little effort to make you sound smart. You knew all along; you're just confirming the obvious. And in the process you transform the person you are speaking to. He too feels validated and that warms his heart. *It's all good*, one little word that might be, in Africa, the name for a swift, striped, gracefully horned animal.

Stille Nacht. Heilige Nacht: a carol to coax heaven toward earth, but how prickly the sound in German, as if a subtext quietly muttered, *Don't believe it*. Like the word *Weihnachten*, Christmas, when we threw sheets over our winter coats and lay evergreen wreathes on our hair and how they stabbed our scalps, making them itch. In our hands, homemade candles, their aluminum holders threaded with wire and tinsel. We sang like angels, walking single file along the icy road after dark. Hair just long enough to sway into the fire behind and, with a snap, flash up in foul-smelling smoke.

Kuchen, Kirche, Kirsch. As if all three were birthed by one enormously pregnant mother—the first named "cake," followed by "church," finally "cherry schnapps." I knew them as the family of K, words that somehow linked human experience: sweet, Godly, sinful. In my mind their alphabetic similarity was no coincidence: the baker spikes the cake, the church welcomes the lost, the blood of our Savior cures despair.

These are words I pack into my suitcase wherever I go. I know them as well as anyone—their shape in my mouth, where exactly each word or phrase is flexible and where not. The feeling they engender is gratitude: so suitable, *my* little words. Have you noticed their engravings? *My* name. But they can be yours too.

Switzerland is a small country roughly the size of West Virginia with twenty-six cantons and four national languages squeezed in: German (64.9 percent), French (22.6 percent), Italian (8.3 percent), and Romansh (0.5 percent), as of 2012. Though German speakers make up the vast majority, Switzerland never had a single language in common. There were Celtic Helvetians and Latin Rhetians 2,500 years ago, then Burgundians, Lombardians, and Alemanni, among other tribes in 400 CE. Even the German-speaking Swiss are not a single group by far. They can, and do, speak standard Hochdeutsch, generally reserved for writing, school, and conversation with foreigners they care to accommodate. But *Schweizerdeutsch* is the everyday speech of all German Swiss. And there are countless dialects in Switzerland. There's Bärndütsch, Baseldytsch, Züridütsch, and Haslidütsch, to name only four. Suburbs of these cities claim their own unique versions, as do wee villages in deep mountain valleys. The distinction between one and the other is occasionally sharp, such that someone from Bern may not understand someone from Zurich (seventy-nine miles away) or Luzern (seventy miles) or the Hasliberg (fifty-five).

Schweizerdeutsch tends to avoid long, intricate sentence constructions. Even when they are speaking High German, the Swiss simplify, cut a sentence or word back to its basics. For example, *Taschenrechner*, or "calculator," becomes *Rechner*. Lukas Mathis, a software engineer in Zurich, points out on his blog, *Ignore the Code*, that there are no official spelling rules for Swiss German—it's a crazy free-for-all when anyone writes in dialect. Thus he advises his countrymen and women to turn off the autocorrect function on their iPhones or they'll be sending texts and e-mails with nonsensical words and sentences.

On Facebook, Ecole alum Benjamin Bächtold posted this, in Bärndütsch:

> *Hoi zäme! zwöi fründe vo mir mache amne wettbewerb mit wome e vier-wüchegi reis dür 2 kontinente cha gwinne. si heis vo 300 team unter di letschte 6 gschafft u si iz uf stimmene agwise. . . . wär easy wener schnäll däm link chönntet folge (http://traintheworld.ch/wanderlust) u für ds team wanderlust (elias & shaun) chönntet abstimme. brucht würklech nume 2 klicks u es würd ne gloubs rächt viu bedüte! Gruess.*

Someone asked him to translate into Hochdeutsch and thus the following appeared after a week or so. Notice the word count: Swiss German (sixty-seven), High German (eighty-one). Which do *you* think is the most efficient?

Hallo zusammen! Zwei Freunde von mir machen an einem Wettbewerb teil wo man eine vierwöchige Reise gewinnen kann die sich über zwei Kontinent hinwegzieht. Sie haben es von 300 Teams unter die sechs letzten geschafft und sind nun auf Stimmen (Votes) angewiesen. . . . Es wäre super wenn Ihr schnell diesem Link folgen könntet: (http://traintheworld.ch /wanderlust) und für das Team Wanderlust (Elias & Shaun) abstimmen könntet. Es braucht wirklich nur zwei Klicks von deiner Seite und es würde den zwei sehr viel bedeuten. Gruss.

And, for the benefit of those who can't read either language, the English translation clocks in at the most concise of all, fifty-six words:

Hey, two friends of mine are taking part in a competition to win a sponsored four-week trip through two continents. Of three hundred teams they are now among the final six and in need of your vote. It literally only takes two clicks, so please follow the link and vote for Team Wanderlust http://traintheworld.ch/en/supporters/add/15207.

One day I set out in search of something to eat, yogurt in fact, the specific flavor *Haselnuss*, which was by far my favorite. Scattered throughout the Bernese Oberland mountain landscape are small markets known as *Lädeli*, pronounced *lay*-di-li. They carry most necessary household goods, cheese, cold cuts, shriveled fruit, and if you happen to arrive early enough, fresh bread and pastries. I'd heard there was one in Wasserwendi, the very next village, just a short walk up the mountain. I hiked around a number of steep switchbacks but found no sight of anything offering comestibles other than a restaurant, closed for the season. Two young men were packing up their compact Renault, ready to abandon their *Ferienwohnung* (*Fewo* for short), or holiday apartment and head down to the city. I asked them, in my best combo of Swiss and High German, "*Grützi. Wissen sie wo der Lädeli ist?*" They looked at each other as if swallowing milk well past the expiration date. They shuffled and swung their duffel bags. Finally one blurted out, *"Was? Was?"* I repeated the word Lädeli, miming the various items for sale there: apple, beer. "Ach, jaaaaa. *Laaadeli* [short a]." The crucial difference was that umlaut. These guys were from Bern. Their home might be less than two hours away, but they didn't get Haslidütsch, even though, once I found it, Lädeli was writ large above the store window.

Dialect is not necessarily just an accent like Alabama twang or nasal Minnesotan. It may employ a unique vocabulary, particular to one region. In the Hotel Gletscherblick, if you prefer your sundae with whipped cream, you say, *Mit Rahm, bitte. Nidle* is both the surname of a famous UFO fanatic and what Bernese citizens call cream. Elsewhere, a foamy cup of coffee without a shred of cream is *Kaficrème*, the last word clearly a swipe from nearby France. Dialect is one way to stick close to home and heart, be faithful to your origins, carve out an identity and differentiate yourself from the rest of the country. It allows one Berner or Basler to recognize another, no matter where they are, using a kind of insider's parlance. Dialect also separates a Swiss German from *ein echter Deutsche*, which considering their history of invasions from the north and east, most Swiss are eager to do. Unfortunately, outsiders might also get the false impression the Swiss are uncultured, less intelligent than the Germans with their seemingly larger vocabulary. In my narrow experience, this is far from the truth. Checking the list of famous natives, there's the architect Le Corbusier, psychotherapist C. G. Jung, psychologist and philosopher Jean Piaget, artist Giacometti, and physicist Albert Einstein, to name a few. And while we're at it, where on these lists are the women? You have to trudge into the twentieth and twenty-first centuries to find evidence of anyone other than Johanna Spyri, author of *Heidi*.

Listening to a foreign language, there should be no laborious, on-the-spot translation, unless you were born with a lightning-quick microprocessor of a mind. And the key to fluency is not necessarily memorizing a long list of vocabulary words, but adopting them organically, one by one, hearing them often, using them often. This way they make a home in the deep fabric of your brain. Lucky the adolescents who find themselves in a new country, surrounded by a dome of strange sounds and intonations. Plenty of opportunity to embarrass themselves. No choice but to jump right in and begin to pull meaning from the air, little by little. Attagirl.

A year went by and my mastery of Hochdeutsch grew. I was classroom proficient, could ask for and follow complicated directions to this or that mountain trail, bus, or train route. At the same time, I tagged along behind Swiss boys, open-eared to the sexy insouciance in their dialects. And the local girls who gathered around the bus stop—their Haslidütsch could be just as reckless, but in intimate conversation it sounded like calliope music, almost Swedish with its lilt and softer edges. Where High German was required, both boys and girls would straighten up, as if facing an intimidating physics teacher and solving a complicated equation. The transformation was complete; even their body language followed. He'd plant his feet and stare straight ahead. She'd knit her fingers together and mature a couple of years. Indeed, beyond mere inflection, the Swiss were lucky to have at least two avenues of speech to suit their behavior.

Back in the late nineteenth century, Mark Twain complained that German was just too polite. Not nearly enough "strong words." Uttering the Lord's name in vain amounted to little more than the upright English "my word!" Swiss Germans have solved this problem; they are brilliant in their profanity and insult. I took home a short list:

Verdami: Damn it.
Gotverdami: Goddamn it.
Gottfriedschtutznocheinmal: Goddamn it, yet again.
Du bisch ein Sau: You're a pig.
Nimm dr chopf/d'händ usem arsch: Get your head out of your ass.
Mütterficker: Motherfucker.
Schafseckel: Sheep's prick.
Schiisdräck: Piece of shit.

And here's the long list, which to my shock and delight I found on www.englishforum.ch, posted by CHexo. Some are pure, nasty-

tempered invention. Many are derived from High German with fabu-
lously vulgar flourishes:

Dräckigi psychopathe sau: Dirty psycho pig.
Läck mer am arsch: Lick me on the ass.
Verfickt/e/s: Fucking. . . .
Saiche: Pisser.
Dubbel / dubbeli: Idiot.
Fick di
Fick di sälber
Ficker
Ficke
Bumse
Schiiser
Siech
Wixer
Sauhund
Dräcksack
Sack
Assi
Esel
Dummi chueh (kuh)
Chueh
Nutte
Schlampe
Tussi
Pack
Yugo
Spermaeimer
Schwanz
Fotze
Puff
Lulatsch
Schofsgrind
Doof

Scheisse
Arschgesicht
Mongo
Behinderet
Schiffe
Pisse
Fetti sau
Fettsack

I haven't translated all of these. Several are, no doubt, misspelled, if there exists a correct spelling at all. But you get the idea. Standing over a shattered mug, the liquid contents of which burned the crap out of your thighs, you have so many choices! Any half-dozen will create a vicious comeback to the gods above, even if the drop was your own *verfickt* fault. Do be sure there is no earthly authority figure in the vicinity.

The experts might say it's better to master one tongue at a time. Forget modern dance till you've mastered ballet. Don't improvise till you can read music. But when you're tugged in two directions, as any adolescent is—Am I child or adult? Follower or leader? Bad girl or good?—the choice is not so simple. The miracle of Swiss versus High German is that you can have it both ways. You can flip from one kind of person to another. You can hang with your homies and please your teachers. You can swear boorishly *and* serve as a fine example for your Kameraden. Care to appear highly articulate or super intimidating? You have the tools. Pluck an Olympic-size word from the air. Impress them. Then right before they roll their eyes to the heavens, let go the sloppiest, salt-of-the-earth, most repulsive insult you can think of. Impress them more.

Warning, the Waters

of Switzerland are deceiving. Glassy brooks slip through pastures and trip down hillsides carrying the invisible filth of cow hooves, but the water is completely transparent; it suggests purity, not poison. A fairy tale lake in bright shades of green appears around the bend of a steep looping trail. You are far from the lagoons of Florida; the little sunset ponds of New Hampshire; the bays of Wisconsin; Martha's Vineyard, Bethany, Assateague—the populated beaches of your childhood. This lake is gem-faultless, polished and gleaming. Look! Heroic nixes are, even now, beckoning . . . vapor shaped and gauzy. They ride the rolling peaks of wind-formed ripples. Pray tell, what century *is* it? Hear them murmur, whispering till they have you doffing your clothes on the pebbled sand, jumping stark naked into their clutches. Your breath is snatched away (sting of a snake, knife cut). Now you stroke faster and faster to keep yourself warm, then slower and slower, floating sleepy now, nodding too far from the shore. Few words are equal to the water's temperature and sensation as it slips over your face. If you froze to death right here, who would care? Would *you* care?

Mediator between hot and cold, solid and steam, conveyor, massager, suicide enabler, tall glass of, mirror, prism, bubble, trickle, boil. . . .

Above the Haslital, waterfalls are slender, unraveling from great heights, like skeins of bone-colored wool. Or explosive, as if bursting from a pipe inside a wall. And all of them slide into the Aare, longest river that begins and ends in Switzerland. Its origins lie in the Lauteraare and Finsteraare Glaciers, west of the Grimsel Pass. The river then turns east toward centuries-old Grimsel Hospiz, once a hostel for miners, now a luxury hotel, then aims northwest into the valley. In prehistoric time, a rugged ridge of Cretaceous limestone arrested this flow until, pounding and grinding, the water sculpted a narrow passageway, a gorge called the Aareschlucht.

Goethe hiked into this gorge in 1779 well before it was safe to do so. He described his experience in the story "Unbeschreibliche Tage." Swiss writer J. Rudolf Wyss visited in 1817 and couldn't help but wax apocalyptic: "In front of you churns the gray-green Aare which appears to be the Acheron at the gate to Orcus; one does not know from whence she comes, one does not know whereth she goes."

For years, the only way to travel between Innertkirchen and Meiringen was by boat through the Aareschlucht. But you took your life into your hands—the river barely three meters wide in spots, swift and murderous. Few ever attempted it. In addition to the current with its sharp turns and whirlpools, there were legends to contend with. In 1814, a Bernese scientist named Samuel Studer reported that villagers had seen a snake called *Tatzelwurm* with a round head and short legs that lived in the gorge. Another man, Vater Hazelstecken, spotted a fat worm with a huge mouth, sharp teeth, and terrible eyes crawl out of prehistory toward him, making a whistling noise. No wonder he bolted for the hills. We needn't worry anymore: this particular creature

Tatzelwurm pastry.

slithered into tradition and now lurks behind glass in a *Bäckerei*, where you can purchase a worm cake, small or "life-size," with pink and brown frosting.

In 1912, a 1,650-meter pathway through the gorge was constructed, connecting the two valley villages, with 400 meters of tunnels and galleries carved out of stone, 1,000 meters of steel bridges with wooden flooring, and electric lighting throughout. A restaurant was added in 1928, renovated in 1987, and this is where you should safely stash your children, each with her very own Ovomaltine and threat, *Nicht bewegen, meine Lieblinge* (Do not move from this spot, my darlings).

Now, go buy your tickets before you change your mind.

Tracing the map with your little finger gives you a false sense of security for the path is longer and scarier than you might imagine, more gangplank than walkway. The handrail rises just above midthigh and steadying oneself means stooping as you shuffle and duck past bowls, chutes, corkscrews, and calderas surging with liquid glacier. Only a few rays of sunlight drop into the crevice before noon. Your sneakers and socks are soaking wet and your hands on the rail stiff with cold. Do the *Wartungen* regularly inspect the bolts and screws? How do the elderly manage this? There are plenty of them in their sturdy Swiss boots and wool pants. What would you do if a section collapsed under the weight of too many tourists? One swell has circled round and round, forming a basin smooth-sided as porcelain. Imagine falling into the whirlpool there. No crack to latch onto, no ledge above or below. Then the downriver sweep, water like an avalanche, rockslide, the ignition of atoms. Unimaginable till now.

To my teenage brain, the thin metal balustrade was more temptation than safe hold. I leaned against it, pushed with my knees, watched my shadow plunge and the water carry me away too quickly for rescue. Not exactly fun, this streak of fright darting from fingertip to shoulder, teeth tingling. Nevertheless, I mentally traced an easy swing of leg over rail, swirl of current like an insane merry-go-round, my arms chopping the air, the seconds later when reason rushes back: *What was I thinking? Was I thinking?* It wouldn't matter a nickel, would it?

Luckily time and yes, the river, rushes beyond my theatrical vision, my conceivable mark in history. It empties and refreshes, unlocks new fragments of rock, pushes the old onto its banks, cares nothing for the wisps of nightmare that settled briefly on its surface, then or just now.

Long ago, the Aare charged from the gorge not, as we might suppose, in a beeline for the Brienzersee but in a helter-skelter sprawl of sinew, vein, and capillary. Scan the flat valley floor and surrounding steep inclines and you'll understand a history of catastrophic floods was inevitable. On the west side alone, three separate waterfalls feed the current: Dorfbach, Mühlebach, and Alpbach. There were countless sodden summers with heavy downpours and rockslides and these were merely the natural factors. In the fifteenth century, the *Kloster* (castle) built a lock in Unterseen, causing the Brienzersee to rise 1.5 to 2 meters. This slowed the flow of the Aare River, transforming most of the valley into marshland. The soil turned infertile; disease followed. Later, hillsides were stripped of trees for the more than a thousand cords a year required to mine iron in Bürglen, Meiringen, and Möhuletal, creating an unobstructed track for cascading water and mud. Photographs and three-hundred-year-old ledgers provide the evidence. But the best proof lies under St. Michael's Church, which sits right next to a slope leading up to the Hasliberg. Here, layers of sediment and rock date back to the first millennium. Again and again, this little church was hammered and filled to the brim with debris from overflowing waters. Parishioners countered with multiple reconstructions over several centuries. In one case, the plaster wasn't even dry before another flood raged through, knocking back years of work.

Correction is the Swiss way, and controlling the Aare became a priority, but only gradually. The most serious water catastrophe occurred in 1762 when debris lay five meters deep in St. Michael's. The Republic of Bern hired Italian engineer Antonio Mirani to draw up a plan directing the Aare's course. But work didn't actually begin until 1866 and took a decade to complete. Meanwhile, there were more floods (1831, 1855, 1860, 1861). In the worst events, water poured steadily through the cracks and windows of houses till the walls trembled and tore away, their inhabitants just barely escaping. Huge trees were uprooted and tossed about. Forest understories, once covered with summer wild-flowers and ferns, resembled moonscapes, as if the carefully tended gardens, village squares, and roadways had suddenly gone to ash.

Water the palate cleanser, recycler, teacher of hard lessons, widow-maker, cloudy, clear, darker, thicker, stranger than any forest or plain. . . .

Today, the Aare travels through the valley in a straight line, firmly banked on both sides by stone and cement. Dogs avoid the gray-green current. You'll never see a canoe or kayak there, never a child perched on the grass, fishing. Too dangerous. Today, mountainside tributaries are hung with wire netting to capture debris tumbling through the falls. Concrete channels are embedded diagonally across steep switchback trails, diverting rainwater into the forest. It's a smaller version of the big Aare corrective, a typically discrete, almost unnoticeable attempt to pre-vent erosion. But in a drenching downpour, rainwater cuts its own tracks across the gravel, dislodging a hiker's purchase, pulling her forward with each slick step. Foolish to think she could walk this path alone.

On the other side of the valley, there's a significant falls called the Reichenbach, bisected midway by an outcropping of rock. Half the water goes left, the other elbows through a circular opening, splaying out like a starched fifties skirt. Both cascades are explosive and toss off tons of splash; water pellets rise like steam and soak anything close by. They are famous thanks to Sir Arthur Conan Doyle, who staged Sherlock Holmes's demise here—his arms locked around archenemy Professor Moriarty as they both fell into the plunge pool below.

If you want to see the place, take the funicular like the old days—a twelve-seater painted bright red with wooden benches, open to the air and heights, unless you prefer drawing the white muslin curtains, neatly tied back with leather straps. Toot toot goes the whistle as the gray-bobbed woman who sells tickets climbs aboard and shifts the train into forward, just like that. No steering required, the angle pre-cisely forty-five degrees, past lush moss-covered rocks and a lick of spray before the falls are even visible. Can it be true—the temperature drops more than fifteen degrees a minute? The falls are now visible, the angle steepening to fifty-five or sixty, the train thumping, tugged by its invisible chain. Someone has nailed two brooms on either side of the track, for what? A little train whisking? You pull into the station, whisked and weathered.

As Doyle writes it, Holmes recognized the feeling of getting close. He was prepared for his probable death with a three-page note addressed to Watson in clear, precise script that declared the following, his final words:

MY DEAR WATSON:

I write these few lines through the courtesy of Mr. Moriarty, who awaits my convenience for the final discussion of those questions which lie between us. He has been giving me a sketch of the methods by which he avoided the English police and kept himself informed of our movements. They certainly confirm the very high opinion which I had formed of his abilities. I am pleased to think that I shall be able to free society from any further effects of his presence, though I fear that it is at a cost which will give pain to my friends, and especially, my dear Watson, to you. I have already explained to you, however, that my career had in any case reached its crisis, and that no possible conclusion to it could be more congenial to me than this. Indeed, if I may make a full confession to you, I was quite convinced that the letter from Meiringen was a hoax, and I allowed you to depart on that errand under the persuasion that some development of this sort would follow. Tell Inspector Patterson that the papers which he needs to convict the gang are in pigeonhole M., done up in a blue envelope and inscribed "Moriarty." I made every disposition of my property before leaving England, and handed it to my brother Mycroft. Pray give my greetings to Mrs. Watson, and believe me to be, my dear fellow,

Very sincerely yours,

SHERLOCK HOLMES

Holmes and his nemesis, "the Napoleon of Crime," struggled momentously at the end of a muddy, three-foot path barely a dozen feet away from the upper falls. Watson described them in florid language (but who can fault him melodrama in a landscape so aggressively beautiful and, quite literally, breathtaking?):

The torrent, swollen by the melting snow, plunges into a tremendous abyss, from which the spray rolls up like the smoke from a burning house. The shaft into which the river hurls itself is an immense chasm, lined by glistening coal-black rock, and narrowing into a creaming, boiling pit of incalculable depth, which brims over and shoots the stream onward over its jagged lip. The long sweep of green water roaring forever down, and the thick flickering curtain of spray hissing forever upward, turn a man giddy with their constant whirl and clamor.

Returning to the scene, Watson found the tragic evidence all too easily: two sets of footprints leading, one way, toward the end of the path. He leaned over the precipice, shouting for Holmes into the broken water.

In the center of Meiringen is a small plaza with a rough-hewn, dollhouse church. The sacristy now serves as a gallery for local artists, but downstairs sits the Sherlock Holmes museum, which opened on the one hundredth anniversary of Holmes's death—May 4, 1991. Its patrons, the Sherlock Holmes Society of London, and Dame Jean Conan Doyle (daughter of the well-known writer) were both on hand to witness the celebration.

A spiral staircase leads down to the exhibits, which include three glass-enclosed cases well stocked with memorabilia, maps, and photographs. Here, the expected hooked calabash pipe and magnifying glass. But, also the *three* hats Holmes wore: a most recognizable deerstalker with its tweed fabric, visor, and flaps; a fedoralike homburg worn on precisely twenty-two occasions; and a black silk top hat for formal affairs. Also of note are items Holmes left at the falls: his cigarette case, several brownish coins, and the note he expected Watson to find, apparently written in pencil. To the latter is pinned an exhibit tag from the British Metropolitan Police.

But what really impresses is the full reconstruction of Holmes's living room or, if you're not swayed by fiction, an excellent fish tank specimen of high Victorian middle-class fashion in London. Best to sit down (a bench is provided) so to peruse each detail without exhausting yourself. I loved the curtains, their valences a faded turquoise with long yellow fringe. Extra lengths of the latter were tacked around the cardboard mantel, surely a fire hazard. The wallpaper was deep blue with busy maroon pattern, chosen to disguise the browning effects of pipe smoke. Then every surface crammed with oil lights, decorative boxes, doilies, Holmes's gloves and top hat, his cast off violin and coat, indicating he'd left in a great hurry. How did anyone move amid such clutter? Impossible to touch every detail with anything but a glance. A terrible thought comes to mind: the room slowly filling with water, levitating chair and sofa, knickknacks bobbing to the surface, and Sherlock's mouth moving like a fish.

Today, the path up to the Reichenbach Falls has eroded from constant pounding and moisture. The precise point where Sherlock fell is marked clearly with a white metal star and a sturdy chicken-wire fence. At night a large spotlight casts what looks like a bumpy crescent moon over the spot, but look a little closer into the shadow half and you'll see it's actually a profile of Holmes, his nose following a small outcropping, the brim of his hat tucked into a cavity. It's both ghostly and kitschy. The fictional character turned to stone.

Unbelievably, there are those who routinely climb this trail. Here's where you can clamber over the fence, jump into the void if you're insane. Here's where I spy with my little eye one of Sherlock's molars in an eddy. The rest of his body has to be there somewhere. Conan Doyle was right to locate his story in this spot, the setting its own turbulent narrative. It's a trap door leading to another layer in the scene: two characters dense with thought, talk, and emotion locked in a tussle to the death. I've never seen or felt anything like it. And to make matters worse, a hot wind of nearly forty miles per hour bullies its way across the falls, hiking paths, and pipe rails, flattening the grasses and forcing trees to their knees.

And me, clinging to anything solid, my forearms threaded with ice and electricity.

Bottomless, borderless, flashing, falling, all matter broken into a million tiny pieces. . . .

In color, water possesses a catalog of hues: gunmetal or pink-tinged gray or evergreen or mint or peacock or ribbon blue, even white. But dip a ladle into the stream, then pour into a tumbler, the liquid will appear colorless. If we could examine the purest sample with aluminum tube, Plexiglas window, and lit sheet of white paper, we'd find only a tinge of blue—water's intrinsic property. This is because water absorbs the reds in our visible spectrum, leaving their complements—cobalt, cerulean, indigo. The thicker the water, the deeper the tint, till deep down we hit black. No light at all. Tannins, released by decaying leaves, can also alter color. Then there are impurities and mineral deposits suspended in water, such as lime, which lead to the bright turquoise of Swiss rivers and lakes. One thing for sure, water does not directly capture its hue from the sky, though we would like to think of sky and water as a pair of cupped hands, cradling, barring us from floating off into space.

Onward the Aare flows straight into Lake Brienz and then Lake Thun; the small city of Interlaken lies nestled in between. Take a boat ride on either lake, but my favorite is the former, its steamboat zigzagging from small village to small beach to the Victorian-era Grandhotel Giessbach, which has its own cog railway and dock. When calm, these waters could be mined and fastened onto rings and bracelets, the color bright, opaque, thick even, like ceramic slip. The only place you can see through to the bottom is around the shore, but it's still not an entirely clear picture. *Milchwasser*, the locals call it, runoff from glacier carrying a cocktail of minerals that give the liquid both texture and hue. Mountains reflected in it gyrate and elongate, lobed rather than sharp. What detritus floats by is scant and well scrubbed: a putty-colored branch, stripped of bark and secondary twigs, is capped by a seagull, who believes he is captain of a slow-moving barge.

The Brienzersee is the deepest lake in Switzerland, but its water is so clean there's little for fish to feed on—no choice bits of algae, duckweed, or even bread washing downstream. Can't have an ecosystem with fish if there's no food for the fish. Hence, only one species thrives in substantial numbers, the Brienzlig. "Do people eat them?" I asked. "Oh yes, but there's never enough for everybody."

Miles later, the Aare horseshoes around Bern, carrying huge amounts of rock flour and snowmelt. Bern is the stately capital of Switzerland, with a stone pit at its core, and inside, real live bears. Once in a while some poor deranged person jumps in. A bear attacks, shaking the victim limp. Shots are reluctantly fired, maiming the city's beloved beast, heraldic from the early thirteenth century.

We think of the urban Swiss as staid sorts—financiers, watch- or peacemakers. But summertime, many of them bodysurf the Aare's icy currents here, despite warning signs along its banks. They strip off jackets and skirts and stockings and ties, climb into swimsuits, and stroll shoeless along the riverbank till they find the right spot to take the plunge. This might be a bridge or high wall or, for the less athletic, a campground where the transition from land to water is less abrupt.

The sixty-two-degree current picks them up and instantly sweeps them away. As if on an ocean, some balance on boards bungee-corded to riverside trees. Banker heads wobble like billiard balls rolling across bright green felt. A leisurely sidestroke is rocket fueled. The fear of drowning is assuaged only by experience—a second or third dip into the river, when the swimmers learn to prepare in advance for their exits and steer from the center of the river toward a well-marked series of steps with vivid red railings, seven in all. One swimmer offered this suggestion if by chance you are sucked into a whirlpool: let the water take you under, down to the river bottom, then push hard, aiming sideways and up. Best to avoid the very edges too, where branches drift and could snag a wayward arm or leg. After the very last staircase, the river constricts and hurls over a dam. Here, you're good as gone, and to prove it, more than a few waterlogged bodies have been pulled out over the years.

The Aare heads northeast through Biel (birthplace of Robert Walser), Solothurn, Aarau, joining and more than doubling the size of the Rhein in the Canton of Aargau. In its powerful new incarnation, it travels on to Basel, where fanatic swimmers and river paddlers take the plunge, despite enormous passing barges. Here, I smoked pot for the very first time with my roomies, Barbara and Anka, and through some fantastic stroke of luck, Tobias. All my favorite people wound up in this beautiful city for a single brilliant day during spring break, and I can't remember how, except that Tobias was supposed to be visiting his uncle, and he certainly made short shrift of that. In the morning, we ambled through record stores, donned earphones, and rocked along with Led Zeppelin, the Who, and Creedence Clearwater Revival. Then we headed to the river at *Mittlere* bridge, where long ago unfaithful women were tossed as penalty for their sins. As one local noted, "They were always thrown into the shallow part of the river and were often home cooking dinner before the husbands realized they were gone." We walked a stone embankment all the way out to an industrial area, where no tourist dared go. There we found the abandoned backseat of some car, and like a genie, Tobias plucked a single tightly rolled joint from his back pocket. Two hits each didn't make for much merriment, but we could pretend. Here's a square blurry Kodak shot of that intense little moment, hair blown wild, the river (let's imagine) a wide green ribbon outside the frame.

Tobias and Sarah in Basel.

The waters flow north through the Netherlands, emptying finally into the great North Sea. Why do rivers flow north? Isn't that against gravity? Why doesn't the sea spill *down* from the north? Questions leftover from my childhood, their answers submerged in decades of facts and features rusty from lack of use.

Thanks to pressure from the Atlantic Ocean, North Sea currents run counterclockwise. The Rhein has little impact on these forces. Its waters are absorbed and carried along with the flow east along the continental shelf. Maybe they'll dive into the Norwegian trench, an abyss plunging nearly 2,400 feet. Or they'll stream over an oceanic landslip and surge upward into a tsunami like the waves that long ago crushed the Faroe Islands or flooded the British coast.

Once upon a time the North Sea was one with the Mediterranean and most of Europe was a scattering of islands. Where were the rivers then? Where did the threads and little scraps of Sherlock's famous hat wind up? Where are the cells from waterlogged loved ones, families long past mourning? Where was the little twig I threw as body double over a guardrail into the whirlpool, where I watched it disappear, instantly dragged down and away?

A river will have answers to your questions and withdraw them just as quickly. On a calm day, a river will reveal your face on its surface, undulant like shimmering heat, banished with the slightest breeze. At night, it will chew on your secrets and those of lives beyond the grave. A river knows you are mostly water anyway and sometimes you wish it were 100 percent. And yet, in times of drought, a river drops, dissolves, and dies into its bed.

I too will die into my bed, as did my mother in her four-poster version, as did Goethe, Sir Arthur Conan Doyle, and Holmes too, though his corpse was never found, as did Robert Walser, whose body was discovered frozen in the snow, as did Vladimir Nabokov in the Palace Hotel, nestled into his valley of exile, Montreux, Switzerland, as did his adored Aunt Pasha back in Russia many, many years ago. Her last words: "That's interesting. Now I understand. *Vsyo—voda*. Everything is water."

Heads Up 〰 *Die Lawine*

Makes sense that nineteenth-century Brits would explore the origins of this word as they explored the formidable peaks in Switzerland, encountering frightening avalanches in their explorations. No doubt a dozen mountaineers were killed off in the process—motivation, at the very least, to wonder about the creature's name. Here, a member of the London Alpine Club records his thoughts:

> It seems evident that Lawine, Lauine, Labine, Lavine, Lavange,
> Avalanche, and probably also Lévantre, Valantre are only differ-
> ent forms of one and the same word. Lavange scarcely differs from
> Lavine, and Lavange, Avalanche, bear the same relation to each other
> as Lévantre, Valantre. The only question is whence the whole class
> of name is derived. The idea is too far-fetched and only a shade less
> improbable, if at all so, than the suggestion that the mythical Löwinn
> (lionness) has stood godmother to the group.

A plummet, drop, dive, sinking in, first round of really bad luck, ruin, dangerous person, one who brings about disaster. Pronounced "lah-*veen*-uh." In the outdated tradition of hurricanes and other storms named for women, the noun is of course feminine, *die* pronounced "dee." Not what English speakers might utter: *die* as in *perish*.

In the Swedish film *Force Majeure*, a family of four lunches on an out-side terrace directly across from a mountain where ski patrols set off a controlled snow slide. First, it's a wondrous event that many of the guests, including the father, stand up to record on their phones. But the catapulting snow veers unexpectedly and tumbles toward the balcony, where a dense white cloud envelops everyone. Panic follows and among the first to run to safety is the father. Though no one is injured, the mother and children are shaken by this man's selfishness and disregard for his family's safety, a betrayal he seems to take lightly. The incident creates a moral divide we're left wondering will ever be repaired.

Would this man have taken it further, casually guided his family into dangerous backcountry where the risk of avalanche grows? It's possible. It's possible even a trusted teacher, in loco parentis, leader of ski tours, director of an eighty-year-plus international boarding school might also for a split second abandon common sense and find himself on violently unstable physical and moral turf.

Cold-hearted lioness, crouched flat against the snow, sights her prey from a ledge above the valley, slowly extends first one huge paw, then another, till she has engaged all four in a furious gallop downhill, a race no mortal could ever escape.

In Transit

Snow and adolescence are the only problems that
disappear if you ignore them long enough.
—EARL WILSON

Once I moved through the air imperceptibly, a four-foot-eleven,
seventy-six-pound feather of a person. By fifteen, I'd sprung up four
inches, altering forever my relationship with my body. At sixteen, I
grew another three. I saw the world through a tiny peephole bored
into the great lump of me—no getting around cumbersome shoulders,
cheeks that loomed like extra noses in my peripheral vision. No super
smooth stride, with heels and soles slapping like diving fins. As my
body rearranged itself, I was forced to think about every square inch of
flesh and let's just say the thinking was dark.

I wasn't alone. Every night K.C. threw himself into an upper bunk,
his puffy comforter collapsing around him, then massaged his legs,
stretching the tissue so it would relax and give way. He was amazingly
limber—he could lock his elbows behind his head—but you could tell
his bones ached they were expanding so fast. I watched a doorframe
slam into his shoulder, sending him into a backward spin that made
me laugh. I knew the feeling: the newel post that punched me in the
hip where a purplish mogul rose in a matter of seconds. What was this
sudden clumsiness but a miscalculation of our trending hands and feet
and legs and arms and chest and waist? K.C.'s voice too was caught
in the discomforting in between. High-low, boy-man, sissy-jock,
screecher-crooner, son-dad. Who might be speaking today? At what

crucial moment? My vocal chords thickened into radio fullness, but more gradually. In choir, I stood in the third row, seen and unseen, shape-shifting from alto to tenor and back again.

Teenagers can grow almost as rapidly as a toddler—boys up to five inches a year. Consider as well the ebbs and flows of serotonin and dopamine, which in proper balance contribute to a sensation of well-being, or in their absence, serious agitation. A wicked mixture of hormonal changes pours into the mix. In short, a teenager's body is bustling with more activity than any other time in a person's life. Who, or what, is directing all this? Unfortunately, the management area of the brain—the prefrontal cortex, responsible for making decisions and solving problems—is notoriously underdeveloped in adolescents.

We had no knowledge of neuroscience or hormonal surges. No one explained our dizzying physical metamorphosis—all of it magnified inside the intense, tightly knit atmosphere of an isolated boarding school. No wonder I dreamed swift currents swallowed me up, the ground broke loose in fast-moving patches.

I was navigating a new language too, one that allowed some easy mistakes, often of the sexual sort. Poor top-heavy Jacqueline sitting on the porch steps. "Brush" in German translates to *die Bürste*, dangerously close to *die Brust*, especially in pronunciation. If you know what you are doing, the difference is a subtle flattening of the tongue's edges, and a trill around the *r*. If you know what you are doing. I asked her if I could borrow her breast so I could smooth my flyaway hair. Later, I imagined such a thing and then could not erase the vision of her naked breasts stroking my split ends. I worried I was a lesbian. Or maybe a pervert. Or both. It was possible.

Oh, I was ravenous—for excitement, gossip, and especially for sex. Nothing was more important than "getting experienced," entering a relationship with a résumé of sexual encounters. First base and its well-aimed deep kisses, second base with buttons and snaps unlocked expertly, third base—that land of zippers and whatever appeared underneath. An involuntary laugh in the heat of the moment? A bit of skin pinched as the pull-tab hits the box? Ultimate mortification. I wanted no surprises.

I was drawn to the ice blue eyes, high cheekbones, and natural blush of effeminate boys like Wolfgang and Peter, but also to "real men" like Tobias, Meinrad, or my cousin Dick. These guys stood well anchored, hands curled at their hips, ready to jump if a basketball bounced their way. Their fingers were chapped and thick. Even through saggy wide-wale corduroys, they looked muscular.

K.C. was harder to classify. I was interested in him as in any reasonably attractive boy. Sure, he dressed in desert boots, green lumberjack shirt, and shiny, chin-length hair parted in the middle—the requisite late-sixties look. But K.C. was unique in his appealing sweetness. Maybe it was the slur in his speech, as if he'd just woken from a nap. I remember ramping down my talk, flirting yes, but quieter and certainly not profane. Oh, the way his ears bent toward me. He could move them like a deer in a certain wide-open attention that saw no harm. I remember he liked me enough to give me a little cartoon narrative he'd drawn in brown and red—a caveman's adventures. I found them funny and clever enough to hang on to for a very long time. See?

Did K.C. and I ever kiss? Did he ever hug me with his telescoping arms? Not sure. It would have been awkward. This boy, with his highly developed ability to see a glass half-full, so endearing to teachers, had a difficult time with sex. He'd left a steady girlfriend in D.C., but he was unsuccessful in love for three entire years at the Ecole. The school boosted his self-confidence in all areas but this. After a while he wondered if there was something seriously wrong with him.

Was it K.C. whose breath turned sour with dark chocolate? Was it the tricorne hat he wore all day, or his page costume in our Shakespeare production *Richard III*? A forest green tunic and headband flattening his already severely vertical hair just as frizz was just coming into style. And tights. Tights!

True, he surprised all of us when snow fell fast and hard for twenty-four hours, drifting to five and six footers under the Turmhaus balconies. K.C. was among the courageous few to teeter precariously on a third-story railing, then cannonball, arms tucked around his knees, into the cold stuff below. He popped up with a whoop and lots of applause then scrambled out of the snow to do it again.

Caveman 1, by K. C. Hill.

Caveman 2.

Too late to make much of an impression on me. I remember an abrupt turn in my affection that had something to do with his age (eleven months my junior)—a completely arbitrary and ill-considered something that turned me off in a flash, like skinny ankles or slumping socks or his beseeching posture on the school's rudimentary stage right next to the twisted, tormented King Richard himself. The contrast would have favored the king, played by Sylvain, eleven months my senior, and wouldn't I say yes if he ever, ever, ever asked me to sleep with him? The contrast made K.C. a soft creature, a mere follower of kings. I remember he liked me too quickly and one morning I woke up and couldn't bear the sight of him. I dropped him like a fish.

Q: Is this the greatest cruelty you've ever inflicted on another human being?

No. For three months I served as "older sister" to a fourteen-year-old named Erika, easing her passage into the school. We exchanged letters in advance of her arrival. Her writing was better than mine, but I was the knowledgeable one and thus warned her about the food and showers, extolling the beauty of the mountains. "You've never seen anything like this! Just wait!" I imagined long blond hair, blue eyes, pale Nordic skin, but in fact when she stepped off the bus, Erika was pint-sized, wearing a gallon-sized denim shirt, maybe her dad's. Even her

Caveman 3.

Caveman 4.

moccasins were floppy, stitches sprung and heels worn through. Did I take her awkwardness and high-pitched voice to be a sign of growth arrest? Yes. Did I look Erika in the eye even once? No. Did I ignore her after showing her around and then talk her down to all my friends? Oh yes. Did Erika want to sit next to me and did I tell her "No, I am saving that seat"? Did I want to shove her over a cliff, her social weight unbearable? Did I in fact nudge her off the chairlift as it pitched into the station and watch as she cartwheeled down the unload area, skis, poles, mittens, glasses, and all?

Any adult who's been close to adolescents knows they are bursting with anger, confusion, fear, and need. One will select a murder's runt and peck as if she herself has no weaknesses. Another may have sex with either sex, trying to find out which satisfies more. She will sit at the very edge of a mountain ledge, legs dangling, dreaming her demise with everyone watching, shock moving through the school like a rogue wave. He listens obsessively to songs of doom and addiction: "Sister Morphine," "Paint It Black," "Dead Flowers"? Definitely Rolling Stones. Teenagers are restless, exhausted, and dying to *arrive*. In the meantime, the endless meantime, they self-sabotage with lapses of judgment and snippets of forgetfulness. Always on the verge of that one erroneous footstep, steered in all likelihood by manic joy or its opposite, a serious hangover.

Q: How close did you come to being arrested?

I wrapped in tinfoil a lump of hash the size of a Ping-Pong ball and placed it in my back pocket. Hash was cheap and easy to come by in Alsace, where Barbara, Anka, and I spent a stoned day in the French countryside, rolling down tufted hills, sleeping in pastures, throwing fistfuls of hay, our hair tangled with it. The chunk in my back pocket slipped my mind till I approached customs at the border. To the right and left, citizens were emptying their pockets, dumping the contents of purses and book satchels. I carried a maroon-fringed Greek-style bag, which I lay down on the metal table as nonchalantly as possible, trying to catch an official's eye. *Look at my clever face, officers. It's fearless.* I flirted in three languages—French, German, English: "*S'il vous plait tamponner mon passporte? Bitte werden Sie meinen Reisepass abstempeln?* Oh *please*, will you stamp my passport? Even though it's not necessary, yes. I'm collecting them!"

Then carefully backed away till the crowd folded in behind me.

Risky behavior, like sucking on forbidden bidis or hazarding a narrow trail at night, can be interpreted as a necessary evolutionary step toward adulthood. It's *practice* being a grown-up. Every night a girl swallows a Dixie cup of wine so that she can pretend to like the taste when she sneaks out with friends for a forbidden drinking party. A boy chooses the icy slope on purpose and makes it down safely, the run all the more thrilling because it was perilous. He catches a whiff of independence and self-confidence. He also appears pretty damn impressive to a handful of girls milling about. Their fingertips tingle with something other than cold.

Ideally, an adolescent is born with decent genetic material—body type, temperament, flexibility, studiousness—delicately intermingled, but not yet matched to what exists in the world. Ideally, she will fall on the right influences, the right combination of peers and parents, friends and strangers, siblings and teachers. Her maturation will be something wondrous: a continuous flow of small adjustments, outside to inside, and the other way around. The girl will find her matches, complements, and guides. She will feel at odds with what she experiences too—some of it will be painful—but the bending is productive. In retrospect, her progress will appear both brilliantly orchestrated and totally spontaneous. If she is lucky. If the stars align.

Adults with half a mind and a little more heart understand that the stars do not always align, thus they conjure the magical concept *potential*. Potential radiates around the child. It's a concept that buys her time, a hope chest of successes parents can claim, yes, as their own too, compensation for enduring inconsolable infants and lazy preteens. Perhaps their child is shy. Mother and father may assume she is a useful adult-in-waiting. Bright matter bubbles in her brain. One day, a watchful mentor will place a hand at the small of her back and gently maneuver, such that the girl imagines the force is her own. There in the distance is her future, a glittering city beside the ocean. A writing nook that soon will be hers in a nineteenth-century brownstone. A moleskin journal, perfect bound as if her poems were already published. *My own studio, my own book. This is what's next.*

Or dad is unemployed, mom an insomniac, and neither parent can provide the sensitive steerage their daughter needs. Except for basic food and shelter, the girl grows up on her own. Maybe she was cursed with an intense disposition, *born that way*. Dangerous behavior— skateboarding in traffic or stealing from Peoples Drug Store—is no big deal. Any one of these disadvantages need not waylay potential with its sense of latent excellence, its soup of "what ifs." A life could move in any direction: forward, backward, or nowhere at all. And most adults are capable of withholding judgment till all the facts are in. Or at least the children hope so. Potential also implies things are not going so well *right now*, but it's close by, a distant splash of water on the tarmac.

A mother grounds a baby's disorientation by swaddling her, restraining her flailing limbs, holding her together. The rigors and constraints of a Swiss international school will do the same, but the key factor uniting these two strategies is the benevolent presence of adults. Not so very long ago, few teenagers graduated from high school. They assisted their parents in the fields, around the house, or cared for the young ones. Beginning in the 1850s and well into the twentieth century, Swiss farmers relied on the labors of children—their own, and others who were shipped off to the country when parents couldn't afford to feed them. Child labor laws and mechanization have altered these practices, but at least these children lived and worked around adults. Most teenagers today spill into large public schools, with dozens of airtight social societies, occupied exclusively by . . . teenagers. They spend a sliver of time with grown-ups and heaps with other adolescents. They may feel rejected, ignored, nonexistent, or welcomed in, but their socialization depends largely on their peers.

The Ecole d'Humanité, with its unique mixture of progressive education and tightly orchestrated environment, has adults present around the clock. Some teachers arrive during a gap year, not so far from adolescence themselves. Others were hired decades ago and never left, retiring to small *Hütten* within walking distance. Some raise their families on campus, with other teachers forming a second and third ring of support as their offspring hit puberty. They all live in close proximity to students in dorm bedrooms or attached *Wohnungen* (apartments).

Humility is the only possible attitude for the educator, who is aware that his or her efforts can fail, that all education is based on hope and not on certainty. Teachers are seen not as purveyors of eternal truths descended from heaven, but as negotiators of compromise forged with subtlety and creativity.

In addition to the daily Mini-Konferenz, there's a weekly pedagogical meeting when the accordion door in Speisesaal is again pulled shut. A dozen Mitarbeiter in parkas or cardigans are seated around a large table. Enclosing them, another circle, every inch of floor space taken up with chairs and shoulder-to-shoulder bodies. (The ratio of teacher to student is one to five.) Frau Riemensberger knits an off-white scarf in the European fashion. Frau Eisenhauer mends a pair of linen pants. Lars flips through a *Newsweek*, and other faculty confer in twos or threes, settling who will present what issue and how. Armin jiggles a miniature cowbell and the patter quickly dies down. The language is

German, though a quiet translation into English runs throughout with two or three younger teachers leaning in to listen. Again, an agenda with various items under discussion:

- Luca is far too fluent in English. Does anyone have any ideas about where he goes next? I fear he will be bored.
- We are inviting women, or should I say "all of female descendants" to come together at Haus am Bach to band together and feel good. Tumble of laughter, as one teacher speaks up: "We are *all*, male and female, descendants of females!"
- Can the olive green notebooks (self-evaluations by students) be moved to next week instead of tomorrow? Several "hear hears" and murmurs of assent.
- I would like to express my concern that Sergei has not been in my class a lot and should be; he's not doing well at all and has lots of illnesses with excuses from his parents. Sometimes he shows up in blacksmithing but takes forever to finish a small project. He's very distant in our family. It feels like he's ready to leave. (Yes, indeed. Turns out he's on the waiting list for another school.)
- Ander's parents own a vacation home here in Goldern and students are using it to break the rules. Sabina admitted to smoking. Fourteen-year-old Christophe had a beer. It was his birthday and he said he had the right to drink a beer. Tessa had one sip. Does that count? Said she doesn't want to be in a school that accuses her. Directors look grim. In the next few days there will be individual sessions with the students' family heads, teachers, and parents. Then more discussion, finally the difficult decisions, yes or no. Tears, profanity, doors smacked into their frames, or a much lighter sentence—a period of reflection with no privileges.

Darning needles stashed in plastic bags. Scarves and hats scooped up from the floor. Discussion peters out like the last bits of liquid from a pitcher. There's never enough time and always more to deal with when Armin looks up and signals the hour.

As they file out and scatter across campus, the faculty keep foremost in mind their students' best interests. And yet, even with impeccable guidance, a teenager cannot rely on adults to become the person she will become. She walks a shifting ground between absorbing that grown-up point of view and vigorously rejecting it. Ultimately, identity and self-assurance must come from within and the path forward is fraught and rarely straight. The term "identity crisis" is attributed to Erik Erikson and first recorded in 1954, the year I was born. It was one explanation for an adolescent's wild swings in behavior, as she tries to integrate her "ideal" self with what others think about her, all the time enduring those turbulent physical changes. The roots of the word *identity* are in the Latin *idem*, from *idenitum*, "over and over," or "sameness" (think "identification" and "identical"). The goal, however, is not to become *like* everyone else but to gradually develop a *seamless* self, composed of all sorts of influences from peers, teachers, relatives, bosses, books, music, film, and so on. A girl watches her friend Vicky execute a complicated Turkish folk dance wearing slippers woven from straw, with turned-up toes. She thinks, *I will fly to Istanbul in the summer and dance. School is just the beginning, a brief stay in my travels throughout the world.* She peeks into Rudy's dorm room, where he lies on a cot, blanched and sweaty, bone erupting from his shin like a fork. She swears, *I will never let that happen to me. I will set my bindings loose and stick to the beginner slopes. Hiking will become what I am good at. I'll have hair like Ioanna's and tie it back with a bandanna.* Her brain is a fluid and highly chaotic place, where stimuli pour into consciousness from all directions.

It's no surprise most adults recall more from their adolescence than any other stage in their distant past. There's even a physiological term for it: the "reminiscence bump," which in graph form stands out as a near replica of the Wetterhorn viewed from the south.

Memory storage varies through time. Very little endures from the toddler years, but as we approach puberty, our recall kicks into high gear. Novel experiences trigger a more elaborate encoding process; events are embossed onto our brain in greater particularity, recalled more easily during adulthood, a relatively stable period of life. As our sense of self develops, there's further motivation to select and stamp and store life occurrences, integrating them into the grown-up story of who and what we are.

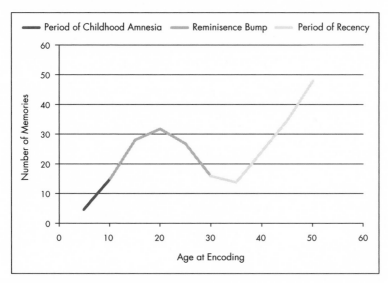

Legend: Period of Childhood Amnesia • Reminisence Bump • Period of Recency

Y-axis: Number of Memories (0, 10, 20, 30, 40, 50, 60)
X-axis: Age at Encoding (0, 10, 20, 30, 40, 50, 60)

Lifespan Retrieval Curve.

Until then, a teenager idles in a physical, emotional, intellectual, and spiritual limbo often accompanied by unbearable longing. As C. S. Lewis has said, "We can be left utterly and absolutely *outside*—repelled, exiled, estranged, finally and unspeakably ignored. On the other hand, we can be called in, welcomed, received, and acknowledged. We walk every day on the razor edge of these two incredible possibilities." My subconscious translated this in-betweenness to dreams of travel, of airports and train stations, of scattered clothing shoved haphazardly into suitcases, of passports gone missing and purses stolen, of interminable waiting, waiting, waiting—sensations so acute they have lasted a lifetime.

One chilly morning on the Sportplatz, as we loitered in small clusters, a rumor surfaced that teachers would be further limiting our free time. Oh, this had gone far enough. What had we done to deserve this? I squawked in protest, encouraging the other crows in my murder to do the same. We were individuals with rights too. We'd swarm into the Konferenz; submit a petition signed by every student in the school, even the helpers and cook staff. So righteous! All this as Herr Gabriel strolled by, overhearing our backtalk. He said nothing. We hardly noticed him, a passing shadow on his way to Konferenz, where surely he reported the whole scenario to the sound of clucking tongues and deep sighs. Not the first such incident for Fraulein Sarah; her conduct has fallen into a disagreeable pattern.

It was a real eye-opener, the fence at a field's far edge marking the limits of what I understood about progressive education. I was not free to express my opinion in this manner. I'd taken, as truth and righteousness, the fire that surged in my chest and could very well have originated in nothing other than PMS. I'd protested without checking my sources. Worse, I'd infected a handful of otherwise well-behaved students. This was not leadership; it was a tantrum. Decades later, I don't even remember if the rumor was true.

No matter, I was placed on probation with a curt note of warning sent to my parents. Even worse, my secret crush Sylvain typed the letter since he was serving as Natalie's secretary. Most admired young man, king with the hunched shoulder, lover beyond my reach, spelled out every single word, including "show off," "disappointment," and "dangerous path." My self-guided experiment with leadership, so blunt and wrong-headed, was quickly cauterized, switched out and replaced with, well, something more grown-up. It was not a difficult transition, a minor adjustment resulting in a new and improved version of Fraulein Sarah. *OK, I get it. I live in a community. I can be responsible too, the type of girl teachers can trust. I'll major in education and become a teacher myself, maybe even here. This is what I am destined to be.*

My parents would be pleasantly surprised when I flew home for Christmas. But who would greet them at Dulles airport in the spring?

Bites ᴧᴧ *Bündnerfleisch*

Only a few countries offer *Bündnerfleisch*, *Bindenfleisch*, or "bound meat," most commonly consumed in Switzerland. Tendons and fat are removed from a cow shoulder, the meat soaked in wine, onion, salt, and herbs, then placed in airtight containers and stored for three or more weeks at a very cold temperature. Finally, it's hung to dry in well-circulated air, pressed and re-pressed to release any remaining moisture.

To serve, slice wafer-thin and arrange artfully on a plate, circular like zinnia petals or the leaves of an artichoke. Or try slivers laid down in shingles, a chevron pattern. If you're alone—no wolf in sight and no danger of forfeiting your share of the treat—savor one piece at a time. The flavor moves along the sides of your tongue with little salt sparks, landing in the center with a beefy, winey rush. Let it rest there. Chew slowly, as your teeth have no taste buds and you want the floating pleasure to last forever.

Dean & DeLuca (New York) carries the product in its deli section at a very high price. See the following link for a video of Switzerland's finance minister Hans-Rudolf Merz laughing uncontrollably at the mention of Bündnerfleisch. If you mix the highly technical parliamentary language of taxation and European Union regulations with the fleshy, sadomasochistic undertones of "bound meat" it's an understandable reaction.

http://www.youtube.com/watch?v=E5agWxzWTsc

Frau L.

The course begins in a way that ignites the curiosity and wonder of the students and encourages them to become actively engaged with the topic. Students have adequate time to finish work at their own pace. They are allowed to approach a subject from several different angles. Simply stated, all methods are supported that further active participation and independence and open up the path to learning and discovery.

English teacher Natalie Lüthi wore her hair tomboy short, in gentle waves, but gentle is not the first descriptive that comes to mind. Her mouth ran a thin, somewhat severe line across her jaw. There was a light tea stain on her temple, nearly concealed by a pair of tortoise shell glasses. Her physique was attuned to steep paths and considerable distances: strong, striding, casual. And I rarely saw her in a dress. A jumper perhaps. Or maybe a Swedish-style sweater and A-line skirt for Sundays.

Oh, she was formidable—fluent in German, Swiss German, English, and maybe French, I wasn't sure. Founder of the international Lüthi-Peterson Camps, director of the Ecole's American division, the driving force behind the school's thriving Shakespeare theater program, wife, Familie "mother" of two dozen Ecole students, biological mother of four, one of whom was still in diapers. Medals prominently displayed on the overcoats of captains and generals were absent on hers, unless you begged her for a story. Could she be persuaded? Not by me. Too shy. Natalie's character matched her appearance: task-oriented, resolutely practical, not a jot of conceit.

The first day of school, the entire Lüthi Familie went blueberry hunting in the mountains. In one luscious spot, the bushes crowded around a boggy pond, which was itself surrounded by evergreens. The pink blooms had long disappeared; branches were fully leafed out. It was the height of berry season. Mostly the fruit was hidden and students plucked gingerly, consuming half of what they harvested, their tin buckets slow to fill. Occasionally, there were dense, weighty clusters. Natalie aimed for these, crawling on her hands and knees, nibbling at the plants with her teeth. *With her teeth*, for grazing was the most sensible way to eat and she cared not what she looked like—lips, tongue, and teeth stained bright purple with slightly lighter shades from chin to nose. Her hands were clean. I stopped in my tracks, staring at this most revered teacher and Direktor. Was she super efficient? Or just *crazy*?

Not surprisingly, Natalie was impatient with pomposity. Paul Geheeb's educational philosophy boiled down to four words: *Werde der / die Du Bist*, borrowed from Pindar, and adopted by many a philosopher and writer since. "We are what we repeatedly do" (Aristotle). "We are what we think" (Emerson). Though some say the expression can be traced even further back, to Buddha's *Dhammapada*.

Become who you are. The phrase appeared in Geheeb's letters and throughout Ecole literature—nothing if not sacred. "Oh, and by the way," Natalie once exclaimed, "what exactly does THAT mean?" She wanted specificity, something a teenager could grasp, a kind of road map for the development of character. Kierkegaard might have whispered in her ear, "Who would take the pains to waste his time on such a task?"

The point, perhaps, is to become what we are not (yet), for what *are* we if we haven't yet become who we are, or never do? Are we trapped at some infantilized stage? And what happens to that early person if we *do* become who we are? Is she shed like snakeskin? Does she dive deep into her brain only to emerge later, during some terrible moral and intellectual breakdown?

In Konferenz, Natalie would half listen while a teacher who favored "big thinking" rambled on, his speech ballooning with elevated language and digression. She'd interject, "What are we talking about?" sometimes jumping in too early with her skepticism and dissent. Armin might have to say, "Come on, give the guy a chance."

But isn't it true, any group of adults gathered for collaborative decision making—brainstorming, negotiating, compromising, planning, evaluating—should have a Natalie in their midst? How else would we get anything done? Natalie did not believe in waste of any kind. She dismissed phatic talk. Her letters to parents were typed over medical records, résumés, extra copies of published articles, mimeographed theater playbills, even sheets of piano music. Every scrap of paper put to use. Every minute spent industriously. All her correspondence opened in similar fashion: *I have a moment to spare, just a quick note before I head into class.*

Once upon a time there was an only child named Philipp Hostettler who lived in a large castle in Bern. His mother fled to Germany shortly after his birth, and his father wasn't much interested in raising the boy, so the responsibility fell to his grandparents, one of whom was a highly successful industrialist who happened to be acquainted with the progressive educator Paul Geheeb. The family enjoyed a luxurious life—servants, fancy cars—and Philipp, who had few limits or rules, turned spoiled rotten. He'd already been expelled from several private schools for wild behavior and mediocre academics. Yes, there were tutors, but they seemed more interested in the many artists and writers who took up residence in the castle. Grandfather peered into the future and decided they'd never be able to handle the boy as they aged, so perhaps Geheeb's Ecole d'Humanité might be just the thing—a kind of exile from the good life, a place to grow up a little.

Philipp rode up the school driveway in the backseat of a long black limousine and everybody stared. His chauffeur ran around the rear of the car to open the teenager's door, carried his ski equipment, bedding, suitcases, and bags of books down a narrow side road (where the limo couldn't pass), dropped everything outside a yellow stucco building called Haus Pöschel, then walked back up the road, turned the limo around, and retreated to Bern. The boy's room was minuscule, without heat, and no butler to prepare his breakfast or lay a nice fire. He would stay here for an entire trimester and deal with it.

Deep down, Philipp longed for comfort, especially of the maternal kind. So he asked to be placed in Armin and Natalie's family and live in their house. But the only special treatment he received there was even more challenging. She woke him well before the gong, when he joined a dozen other young boys from the *Holz* or *Sportgruppe* clearing the woods behind their house, where a new set of dorms was to be built. And thus began his passion for carpentry. Later, he even built a sled entirely from scratch.

In the winter, there were English lessons. He must handwrite a short but grammatically correct paragraph: instructions for riding a bike or a synopsis of a scene from Shakespeare. Later, in preparation for his role in a play, Natalie drilled him till he could recite the lines in his sleep. As the only family member who didn't speak English, he had to be brought up to snuff, and fortunately, the reward for all this predawn activity was a breakfast of Rösti and eggs, personally prepared in Natalie's kitchen. Philipp hobbled into the apartment exhausted but freshly showered, hair slicked back, and famished. It took almost a year, but the woods were cleared, the eggs scarfed up, and best of all, Phillip began to take his studies more seriously.

This story wasn't particularly apocryphal or even unusual. Most students who lived or studied or worked with Natalie knew she was a kind of supreme magician who took on a number of the most difficult kids and turned them around. A few were intimidated beyond hope, some buckled under her expectations, others gave up and gravitated to other faculty, but almost everyone remembers this teacher as the single most important influence in their adolescence.

Natalie's English classes were held in her Westhaus apartment. The room was always a little too warm, scattered with straight-back chairs and lots of silk-screened pillows, large and small. It was privileged space. Absent were the middle schoolers, banished their immature taunting and bickering. Twelve or thirteen upperclass students quietly leafed through paperbacks and three-ring notebooks, alert and pleased to have finally landed in this intimate circle. Conversation stopped abruptly as Natalie slid into her window seat. Respect was in the air.

An excellent teacher makes useful every minute of time and expects her students to be prepared. If the task's a pop vocabulary test, the quizees get ten seconds per word to think and write. If we are in act 2, scene 1, of *Richard III*, parts are assigned at random and the read-through begins immediately. Most steer through the thick, seventeenth-century diction with ease, but here's a girl who should be more fluent. "Come on," Natalie says, her irritation rising. "Do you even understand what you're saying?" That afternoon, the girl spends her free time perched on a big rock up the road, practicing tomorrow's scene till she has it down. Thanks to her poor performance, she may never again be chosen to participate, but she can't take that chance. She then reviews N through O of her vocabulary words and returns via cow path, where she sees a half dozen Americans dotting pasture and woods doing the very same thing. They look like a widely dispersed picnic, one without food, drink, or pleasure. Forty years later, she still can recite Richard's opening monologue with feeling.

Other than quizzes in preparation for the big mother of all, the SAT, there are no exams in Frau L.'s class. One week, *Our Mutual Friend* is assigned for discussion. *A Midsummer Night's Dream* the next. "Source Theme" takes an entire trimester. Break down the overwhelming task of writing a thirty-page research paper into smaller chunks. Reading, underlining, note cards, outlines, first draft, second draft, finished copy. I had no problem choosing a subject. Like many teenagers, I was enchanted by psychological deviance, specifically early childhood autism, and so placed an overseas order for Bruno Bettelheim's *The Empty Fortress*, which became the primary material of my paper. An early propensity for *Alles in Ordnung* (everything in order) made the process intensely satisfying for me. My notes were tidy and particular. I spread them across my blanket like a royal family tree, where abstract ideas were kings and queens, backed up by dozens of leafy offspring. Bettelheim compared autism to being a prisoner in a concentration camp (he was himself a prisoner at Dachau before World War II) and espoused the theory of the "refrigerator mother"—who held her infant but did not look at her, who spoke with animation to others but never to her child, who preferred bottles to the breast and baby swings so she could safely leave the room and run the laundry. Thus the child never bonded and withdrew into an antisocial state, displaying a series of repetitive behaviors that no one around her could possibly understand. Bettelheim's book was key in this widely accepted explanation for autism during the sixties and seventies. The theory has long since been discredited. Still, I was fascinated. I wasn't autistic. But maybe I could suspect my mother, and her mother before that, and yes even Natalie for at least *some* of my personal problems.

Frau L. checks in at each stage, comments quite specifically, and will not let students move on till they are proficient. Note that forward progression rests mainly in the student's hands. The good teacher merely turns the key and operates the gate. If she notices talent along the way, she faintly approves, and the student learns to savor the tilt of her chin or barely perceptible widening of her eyelids. Once, I felt bereft of these small appraisals and so, stood outside Natalie's office door, dry mouthed and sweaty, till I finally knocked. I'm not sure where I got the courage to do this, but an elated letter to my parents followed quickly.

I had delivered a mere fraction of my sad little story, when in true form Natalie interjected, "Are you kidding? Any adult around here knows that if they want to get something done around here, you're the go-to person." Then she rustled through her papers and, wagging a sheaf of them inches from my nose, assured me that if the Ecole gave grades, in English I'd have an A. Natalie's hand, which had steered so many young people in the right direction, settled in the small of my back. But it was Sarah who took the first frightening step.

I was placed in charge of *Putzpausegruppe*, making sure all 150 kids were assigned the right 150 chores. Some "mature" Kameraden made use of this position to favor their friends and punish their enemies. I stashed a little memo pad in my jacket for dutiful notes, recording teachers' requests, eager to please—"Put Heinrich in Waldhaus with me," said Herr Cool. "I should keep an eye on him." Frau Durst: "Feli's become a real hypochondriac. Give her an outside job." K.C. and his

Dear Mom and Dad,
I talked to Natalie last night. God,was I nervous..I began my
speech and she interupted me right after I said that I had felt
that my academic situation was at loose ends and that I felt the
my strong points had suddenly become weak points. She asked me
if I thought I knew why. I couldn't say to h er face that I
thought it was her form of teaching(that I can't say is true
anymore as I just got back a paper,with a whole paragraph of
praise) I said I thought it was that I'm am so used to being
the top of the class,and all of a sudden to have kids in the cla
ssroom who are so much smarter than I am,made me loose my head.
She said tht forx source of confidence,is a very temporary and
unsure one and that I really should find another source. She
was glad that I was realizing all this. When I said that about
my position in the class being so unsure,she said that my positi
on was the most sure (on the outside)that she had ever seen ,
and that my writing was extremely clear and logical. I just sat
back there and couldn't believe my ears. All this time I have
just been assuming the worst. She had been wanting to talk to
me about my "leadership". That has been half of my insecurity,
having the sehnsucht,the initiative to do something about the
school and yet to be so frustrated. Howlong have I wanted to be
in the Student Council.and how long has someone else always
gotten in,and how long have I waited to have someone suggest me.
I have completely lost my confidence as a leader,because as
soon as something.some good idea pops into my head,it is always
just dropped. Natalie said she had been considering me a long
time for the president of the course planning group. It is a
hell of a job,but she feels that I can do it.

Letter to Mom 2.

friends got *Abwasch* for the hilarious water fights, which didn't go over well with the kitchen staff, but no matter—they'd clean up. Any loathsome leftover tasks like mopping the heavily trafficked hallways I awarded to the brownnosers and loudmouths. I was no saint.

Taking responsibility for the welfare of the community occurs when a stu-dent takes on the leadership of a project: tending a booth at a festival, tutor-ing a younger student, or bringing sick people their food. Success in a small project like this gives students the courage to undertake bigger projects, and their self-confidence grows. Such experiences of success in the adolescent years are crucial for the future adult in his or her ongoing journey of "becoming who he or she is."

If you happened to be in Lüthi family, you were treated with impec-cable fairness, or so the theory goes. Certainly Natalie was an atten-tive family head. Every morning before the gong sounded, she moved through the house opening windows to let in *die frische Luft* and hov-ering inches from our comatose faces to chirp *"Morrrrgen!"* At one point we "children" numbered twenty-four, the largest *Familie* ever. Sometimes she and Armin retreated to their apartment and had a quiet breakfast with their genetic offspring, Piet, Chris, Molly, and Doey, but no one could blame them for that.

I remember Anise, placed under Natalie's care seemingly without discussion as soon as she arrived from Argentina. What else could account for the fast track other than Natalie's head-over-heels infat-uation with this blue-eyed, straw-haired teenager dressed in brightly embroidered pants and poncho, native of South America—well below the equator, halfway around world? They cooked together, sat close in the Speisesaal, and Anise tagged along testing her Spanish vocabulary as they marched up the gravel road to Westhaus. Several months later, I passed the poor girl in the hallway, sitting knees to chest against the wall, utterly crushed. Natalie had dropped her like a worn penny. No question, I thought, Anise was irritating with her constant good cheer and national pride. Still, I couldn't help but wonder: Is an adult allowed to behave like that?

Female students occasionally grumbled that Natalie "preferred her boys." Creighton, Sylvain, and my cousin Dick were among these anointed fellows. K.C. was singled out early, his matriculation into the Landerziehungsheim lovingly shaped by close contact with the Lüthis, especially Natalie. And once during a Christmas conference, everybody stared as Frau L. and Dan, another of her unabashed darlings, danced the hambo in Turmhaus's auditorium. The Riesling flowed, the floor was crowded, but they were the ones to watch. Such merriment in their faces and obvious pleasure in each other's company and arms! We imagined they were in love—Natalie two decades older—and perhaps they were.

These were interesting complications, little transgressions that I stored way back in my brain. Somewhere in every grown-up, there's a scintilla of frivolousness, even unsafe behavior. We'd seen her cruel and certainly a little drunk. What did she dream about? Did she ever fumble or stutter? Was she ever untrue, misguided, reckless?

For the most part Natalie had an uncanny ability to know just what to do for a lazy, rebellious, or underappreciated kid. Even on her deathbed, she lay seemingly unaware until one of her surrounding family and friends mentioned a particularly sad situation with this boy or that girl. She sat right up and asked, "Who's suffering? What are we doing about it?"

Training for responsible adulthood—for responsible citizenship in democratic societies—begins in childhood with exposure to democratic structures in daily life. Old and young members of our community attend the weekly assembly, where everyone has a voice and can bring up issues and concerns for discussion.

I completed my sophomore year with several minor community tasks under my belt: prompter for the annual Shakespeare play, volunteer for the student council, and so on. At the end of every trimester students reflect on what they have achieved in each course period. An hour is set aside, sometimes on Saturdays, when the *olivgrünen Hefte*, or olive green notebooks, appear in a neat stack, along with a bundle of sharpened number two pencils. Inside, students measure their positives and negatives in thoughtful consideration. They can be as open as they wish. Comments are meant to be specific, completely honest, and to make sure, teachers are not allowed to read the notebooks. The idea is to instill a bit of soul-searching.

Alas, the tradition was in decline. Maybe a teacher got wind of a growing revolt. Someone surreptitiously plucked notebooks from trashcans and found all too many illustrations, cartoons, and more than a few wiseass "appraisals": "I did great. I'm the best one in the class. Herr Kohl is the stupid one." All I know for sure is this: One afternoon, Natalie stopped me in the hallway with a thought: "Hey wait. Why don't you revive die olivgrünen Hefte?"

We don't need to be told that strong emotions add weight to a memory. When we experience any high-octane event, the memory is transferred quickly from short-term to long-term storage, where it endures, seemingly, for a lifetime. Traumatic experiences are doggedly persistent, rematerializing in our dream *and* waking lives. It must be noted, however, that the only details a girl remembers are her own details, not those of people around her, and not necessarily the facts.

The olive green notebook revival was a modest, but reasonably above-the-radar project for a sixteen-year-old and her growing sense of responsibility. From Natalie's point of view, I'd make a fine example to other students, adding (conveniently) a society-friendly activity to my college application. I wrote a small speech, emphasizing the unique opportunity: Students have permission to say something constructive about their classroom experience without being judged! All those under-the-breath mumblings and those inner doubts can be voiced, clarified, put to some use, especially if the student is willing to share them with the class, or even the teacher. Few other schools allow this; we should be grateful for the opportunity. My roommate Claudia helped me translate a couple of paragraphs into German and I spent two or three days rehearsing in the bathroom till I could speak without notes.

Schulegemeinde was our weekly community gathering, conducted in German, under the direction of Herr Lüthi. Here, student petitions could be presented: a *Tanzabend* (rock 'n' roll dance evening) every

Saturday instead of once a month, or more hot showers, or record players in dorm rooms, or the elimination of Morgensport. Before stepping into the large auditorium, we often met in the run-down shack Baracke and hashed through our arguments. It was hardly an efficient process since there were no obvious leaders, but this too was an important lesson, that a free and open democracy requires some limiting factors (governance, rules) if anything is to happen. Alas, I lacked the foresight to call a meeting in Baracke or my dorm room or anywhere. It would have been a fine place to practice my speech, not to mention determine how my comments would go over.

The thud of boots over wooden floors and chairs scraping and boys jostling each other came to an abrupt close as Armin raised one finger and spoke, "*Ruhe bitte.*" Announcements came first. The workshop in clay will meet downstairs in Max Cassirer Haus while the kiln is installed. Sign-ups for Shakespeare end tomorrow. A group of Swiss psychologists will be visiting classrooms, so please be on your best behavior. The advanced ski group will be skinning up to Planplatte if anyone is interested in joining. Someone has stolen twenty francs from Peter Feldbaum's locker. The village Lädeli is not a place for roughhousing or swearing and the like. Then Armin turned to me, pronouncing my name like a drumroll: *Saaah*raaah?

Was that the best he could do with my name? Why was he dragging those long vowels around the room like a Turkish sultan? Someone giggled. No matter. I stood up and, addressing no one in particular, delivered my pitch with impeccable pronunciation and great feeling. My voice sailed without a shred of chop. My hands kept their secret, nested behind my back. I'd outwitted my body's automatic tendencies, managed, in fact, to appear bodiless. All message. I sat down, relieved.

Did I think I could now sink back into the crowd, disappear behind the students crowded around me, slip blissfully into their cocoa breath and comforting indifference? Was this some kind of irrefutable announcement like the ones Armin had just broadcast?

No. As it tends to do, time moved on and conditions were about to change and an infinite variety of outcomes were possible beyond the one I had foreseen. Why had I *not* braced myself for the unpredictable, the simple fact that my speech prompted a response, an argument, or at the very least a lively, off-the-cuff discussion.

Herr Brabant stood up—native of Munich, distant relation of Himmler perhaps, except that he was cerulean-eyed and devastatingly handsome, popular with children, an easy-going teacher. In fact, he had trouble controlling *his* classroom. His beautiful head pivoted about; he took in the entire scene, a background in theater obvious. Now he circled back to me, enunciated a few clipped sentences, voice rising slightly toward the end.

A question.

We're familiar with the conductor who faces the orchestra and lifts his hands to begin the first movement. Trills of violin die down; the flutes arrest their scales. The silence marinates ever so briefly and everyone is alert. But what if his hands froze like that, suspended in jaw-dropping quiet. An extended, disquieting quiet?

Though Brabant spoke immaculate Hochdeutsch, I cannot tell you what he said. I wish the question had streamed into my mind slowly, my command of the language secure enough to instantly translate. No, this was a waking performance dream. I shrank inside my clothes or they fell away, it was possible. My chest flamed. My tongue slid and sucked over my front teeth, seeking out a spinach leaf or seed wedged into a crack. The little speech, typed on its scrap of line paper, was now worthless, powdery from so much nervous rubbing.

Natalie was somewhere in the last row, nodding her head like a metronome, counting off the seconds, thinking in her efficient manner of Beckett: "No matter. Try again. Fail again. Fail better." She'd already lined up another task, lower profile no doubt. A handful of my friends had been rooting for me; now they examined their fingernails. The rest of the kids turned to each other with suppressed hilarity, puffs of amusement emanating from the corners of their mouths. I guessed that Armin was vexed, at least for a split second. He too had a way of speeding things along unless it was absolutely vital to linger. With ears ringing and vision narrowed to a pinprick, I waited for the spotlight to migrate to another speaker, another subject. I'd created a moment oozing with confusion.

Maybe my mother could arrange a quick flight home. Surely Swiss Air had a seat on one of its daily flights to Dulles? But long distance was expensive, reserved exclusively for true emergencies. Instead, I skipped lunch, kept to my room throughout the afternoon, and passed on dinner too. Claudia brought me salad and bread and boiled me an egg in her little hotpot. She would tell everyone I was nauseous, which would explain my lousy performance. At least I hadn't strewn vomit everywhere. The next morning, Natalie knocked once and stepped into my room, immune to my swollen eyes and pathetic whimpers: "I think it's time you got over this. See you at breakfast."

Here is a lesson I never expected: Pick any random moment in a random crowd of people. Most are thinking of themselves, attention drifting to thoughts of sex, a chocolate soda in a frosted glass, Bazooka bubble gum stuck to a flip-flop, the long list of things to do next, the should-have-saids, and so on. Knowing this can actually be relaxing.

On the other hand, if you can harness it, adrenaline is not such a bad thing and may actually *help* your performance.

Years later I noticed a Facebook post from Sonia, an old classmate-turned-faculty. She applauded the move from Saturdays to Mondays for the olive green notebooks. A real weekend! No pulling teeth! Indeed, while her students were scribbling, she herself wrote down her thoughts, and later, the class had a superb conversation about what they all liked best about English I and what could be improved. I messaged her: "You mean you're still using the olivgrünen Hefte? I guess that little speech I gave did the trick!"

"What speech?" she replied.

"Become who you are" certificate, signed by Natalie Lüthi-Peterson.

Verrückt in the *Föhn*

The wind grew so tempestuous during the night, and blew in such gusts against the walls, that the hut trembled and the old beams groaned and creaked. It came howling and wailing down the chimney like voices of those in pain, and it raged with such fury among the old fir trees that here and there a branch was snapped and fell. In the middle of the night the old man got up. "The child will be frightened," he murmured half aloud. He mounted the ladder and went and stood by the child's bed.

—JOHANNA SPYRI, *Heidi*

The wind seems to be an undependable blunderer; its lull is as sweet as compliance, blissful in itself, flowering round itself, feeling itself beautiful. Does the wind feel that it is windy?

—ROBERT WALSER, *Speaking to the Rose*

What an odd word. *Föhn*: that boisterous dry downslope wind that occurs mountainside in tidy, neutral Switzerland. Compare it to the chinook (Pacific Northwest), Zonda (Argentina), or halny (Poland and Slovakia). Speaking it aloud, with proper elocution, I sound like Chief Inspector Clouseau impersonating a telephone repairman:

—I am from the telephone company and there is something the matter with your *Föhn*.

—My *Föhn*?

—Hm.

—You said something was the matter with my *Föhn*.

—Yes.

—My *phone*?

—That is correct. That is what I have been saying. Your *Föhn*.

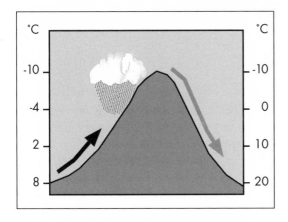

Ideal weather
conditions for the
wind called *Föhn*.

English speakers insert an *e* after the *o* to replicate the miniature
vampire bite mark they call an umlaut, which in this case forces the
mouth into an aristocratic pinch. "Let me tell you about the *Föhn*,"
pronounced "fern," with a British accent, the tongue thrust forward
instead of dropping back to include the *r*. My American friends look
at me Föhney. From whence do *you* come? The source may be Latin—
favonius, or "favorable"—after the Roman god of the warm west wind.
But *Föhn* is a long way from *favonius* in both spelling and character,
as we shall see.

Imagine, if you will, the Hasliberg in winter clothing. Across the valley, on the far or windward side of the Wetterhorn, snow falls in heavy
sheets. Drifts bank against houses and huts. An oncoming wind travels
over this landscape and begins to climb up the mountains, dumping
deeper and heavier snow as it ascends. By the time the Föhn reaches
the top, the sky has unloaded most of its moisture. A broad, horizontal
cloud known as the *Föhnmauer* rises on the backside of the mountains,
visible from miles around. Consider it advance notice. It certainly won't
be long now—time to call in the snowboarders, hikers, chickens, and
dogs. Lock the shutters; make sure the gates are latched.

At first there's a pause, a kind of weather void, and the population
grows restless. As the wind begins its leeward descent toward the
valley below, it is compressed and warmed, gaining speed like a skier

plunging down a jump. Conifers sway and rustle in the distance. They bow in tandem, acres of green-coated monks. The wind charges across the valley and within seconds it's upon us with freaky violence.

Föhn speeds have been known to exceed those in hurricanes, more than 140 kilometers an hour, lifting huts off their foundations and smashing roofs. If there were any streetlights here, they might be flipped sideways to the ground. Branches, whole trees, entire swaths of forest have been knocked flat. I have never seen its effect on water, but I've read Hermann Hesse's novel of a young man from a Swiss mountain village, *Peter Camenzind*:

> The blue-green lake instantly turned ink-black and was suddenly covered with scudding whitecaps. Though inaudible only minutes before, it soon thundered against the shore like an angry sea. . . . Everything appeared to close in—mountains, meadows, houses like a frightened herd. Then the grumbling roar began; the ground trembled. Whipped-up waves were driven through wide stretches of air as spume, and the desperate struggle between storm and mountain rang continually in one's ears, especially at night.

Yet the god Favonius is pictured flying over the grass with a sling of violets and daisies like spring itself. Not the first image that pops into mind watching *this* Alpine wind's advance. Layers of snow are destabilized, icy overhangs fracture and dive into the valley. Sometimes a slope is licked clean. Well, almost clean. More of a mud-grass-pock-marked-ice-mosaic. The air is bone dry and limpid, casting a cobalt light over the landscape. Each rock, pine needle, roof tile appears in high definition.

Special guards, known as *Föhnwächter*, are employed to enforce weather-specific regulations, some of which were established as early as 1736: no baking, no smoking or fires of any sort, especially outside. The dangers are obvious, as fences fall to kindling and hay scatters like pick-up sticks across dry fields. In 1879, wind-fueled fires destroyed more than a hundred houses in the valley village of Meiringen, and yet again in 1891. Still, there are idiots whose lit butts bounce and swirl in the dark, sparks flying. Perhaps they're feeling invincible, aware that some crimes committed during the Föhn are treated with leniency—disturbing the peace, underage drinking, spouse abuse, even rape.

If it bore a mortal shape, the Föhn might resemble a lewd, unbalanced, side-zooming fat man in a big hurry to catch a train. Hey! Watch where you're going! Wind that parts the beaded curtain not with one hand but with its entire torso. Wind that yanks on my ponytail. Rude wind that inflates my shirt and breaches the bedroom and careens down the hallway, rattling doors in their frames and lifting newspapers into a cyclonic spout. A woman sweeps her foyer all day long. Each time someone opens the door, twigs, sticks, shredded leaves, seedlings, and torn bits of paper slip in and land on the Velcro-like carpet. Later we see her with a vacuum cleaner she wears like a backpack, though it too does little against the suck and drive of this Africa-tinged bluster. During the Föhn you'd be hard pressed to find a single open window or door, even if the air inside is stultifying. *Don't let the chaos in* is the Swiss philosophy. Cleanliness first, comfort second.

And what does the wind exact from us? Hair, light scarves, sunglasses, hats, composure. It upbraids and abrades. A mysterious illness surfaces known unofficially as *Föhnkrankheit*. Symptoms include everything from minor headaches to migraines, giddy laughing to psychosis. The suicide rate climbs, as does violence. Animals, insects, even microbes are affected. The culprit is a profusion of positive ions, which wreak havoc on serotonin levels. Scientists now call it "serotonin irritation syndrome" and note that its effects are similar to those caused by long-term exposure to high-voltage power lines.

There will be little academic or agricultural productivity for the next few days. We know this without being told: Weather can wipe out discipline, sanity, and phone lines in one stroke. Weather can force us to our beds.

I remember Cindy with her thick chestnut hair and wide-open face. Reliable, intelligent, clearly a class above everyone else in bearing and thought, but during the Föhn she experienced outbreaks of anxiety, which somehow always occurred in public places. On Sunday, during *Andacht* (the school's devotional Quaker-like service), she swayed and twitched, her emotion so unsuitable no one dared to ask what was wrong or would she like a Kleenex. She wept copiously and we stared at her, entertained by her strangeness. Or we moved away, afraid her disease would rub off. I fell into the latter category, vulnerable to Cindy's slack grip on reality. It might loosen my own. I could be Cindy and she could swallow me. Finally, a friend drew her up by the arms and walked her upstairs. Herr Lüthi finished his reading of Goethe. The rest of us could concentrate now, candles genuflecting when a gust penetrated the double doors.

In this wind, the sensitive girl sinks. The imaginative boy grabs a knife. The dog snaps its leash and runs for the valley.

Once a villager climbed the outside stairs to our dorm and stood at a second story window there, penis in hand, till finally a girl noticed him leering from the dark. He barely flinched, rocking back and forth on his heels, while she was all panic, flying off to find a teacher. The rest of us huddled in the hall, overcome by nausea and shame in our chaste and unrevealing pajamas. By the time the adults arrived, the pervert had disappeared. We knew he hadn't gone far. He wore overalls and red long johns and never was adjudicated. A mother whispered on his behalf into an official's ear, or perhaps a brother vowed to keep a better eye on him from now on and fasten the lock when the wind rose.

A *Trychel* is a cowbell, but not the touristy kind strapped to a cow's neck with brightly fringed collar. No, this one is specifically designed for ritual. Cast iron is replaced by hammered sheet metal, making the huge bell easier to carry by men and boys. In the Hasliberg tradition of *Ubersitz*, they gather and march before weddings, sometimes on Christmas and through the New Year, driving away evil spirits, invoking the good. I've heard of other occasions too, such as long stretches of high wind, when reason wanes and paranoia builds.

One blustery night, dozens of farmers advanced from nearby Reuti, dragging and stomping their boots rhythmically in time with their enormous black bells, which they swung solemnly back and forth. Hardly the random jingle of cattle switching fields—it was midnight,

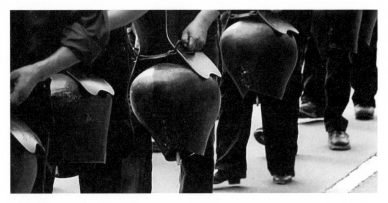

Ubersitz procession with cowbells.

pitch dark, and scary. Closer and closer came the tolling and the farmers, like the pitchfork-carrying townsfolk in *Frankenstein*, till they reached the entrance to our school. There they stood, faces stone serious above their deafening *Trycheln*. The evil they wished to drive away lived *here*, in our modest assemblage of buildings. We were the monsters, tempters, and forerunners of unacceptable change. We had invaded decades ago like a settlement from Mars, and their fear and suspicion, which had simmered long and low, needed little more than this stretch of cathartic breeze to rise to the surface. Plenty of students were awake now and hung off the balconies, transfixed. No one spoke, or couldn't because of the din. This was a mythic standoff between insiders and outsiders, the past and the future.

Finally, Herr Lüthi arrived and spoke to one of the villagers—somehow he knew exactly which one and what to say. They turned around. Gawkers too were shooed off to bed, and some of them slept, though the wind carried on and on into the night.

Oh the flush of disobedience! The weather, with its intense need, calling us outside, undermining our judgment, the perfect excuse for flying into the face of curfews and bedtimes. Better yet, skateboard down a steep mountain road or break into a farmer's shack. Down the *Reutistrasse* we soared, propelled by the wind, forcing us forward into a sprint to the "end of the world," a sheer drop-off and rumored location of suicides. School delinquents loved our company. They led the way. "Here's the spot," they said, peering over a flimsy guardrail to the gorge deep below. "Makes you want to jump, doesn't it?"

Smoke? Roll in the hay?

My sexual activity peaked under these precise meteorological conditions. For nearly a year I'd been mate dancing with Tobias, brushing close in dorm hallways, watching him watch me across the Sportplatz. He wore a tweed overcoat that swung open as he raced to classes late, always late. I adored his blue jeans, worn threadbare at the heels where they dragged over the tarmac, the leather strap he tied around his wrist, and gold puzzle ring. I adored his gravelly voice and belly laugh. I could fall against this boy and he would catch me just by standing there. For a full week, he was assigned wake-up duty, and I joined him early in the morning, striking the gong while dozens of sleepers moaned behind closed doors. Gradually, our social circles merged and he threw an arm over my shoulder while we sat on the dining hall steps and—this was the clincher—was not in the least concerned that everyone around us took note. We were crossing lines: American to Swiss, tenth grader to eleventh, clique A to clique B. For now, he gave up his pursuit of campus queen Ioanna and concentrated on me. My concentration on him was thorough and dizzying. Schoolwork in this atmospheric state was ridiculous.

The night of particular note, we bought a bottle of verboten wine and hiked, holding hands, up to a ridge above the school. We watched the stars blot out as the Föhn moved in and the temperature rose. The Reutistrasse was full of yelping, whooping students, tossing hats and gloves into the air. I held my nose and gulped down my share of *Wein*, gagging with every slug. It was cheap and I had little experience with alcohol. But Tobias was a pro. He finished in double time, belched generously, and bumped my shoulder, spilling the red stuff all over my flannel shirt. This would be a problem, the olfactory *A* wafting past teacher noses, so I wiggled out of it and tossed it into the woods.

Now we were kissing big, wet, drooly kisses. His tongue felt big as a hand. Was I supposed to purse my lips? Were my breasts too small?

Where was my right arm? Should I do something with it? Alas, not yet drunk enough to stop *thinking*. Then we stood up and the 15 percent proof hit me, both of us eager to find a dark corner where we could finish what we had started.

Behold, next to a barn, a lean-to hurriedly constructed of scrap, the farmer obviously sick of rain soaking his firewood. It even had a crooked door with a latch, though locking it meant the funk of hay settled over us like wet wool. Outside, the wind continued to knock. Tobias pushed me toward a pile of kindling and reached clumsily into my pants, no contraception in mind, just sex, his middle finger groping, and both of us groaning like we were supposed to, like we wanted to, in a great grand hurry to go all the way. First, second, third base . . . nearly home and totally hot.

But just as Tobias reached for his zipper, the door exploded. And it wasn't the Föhn; it was our twenty-something English teacher, Richard, who stood there for a second, his mouth tilted into a smirk, before he solemnly pulled us out into the street and marched us off to bed, gleefully enforcing his idea of sanity. There would be dues to pay. We didn't care. The alcohol blazed and the air messed with our faces and brains and I was rhapsodic as if I'd climbed an impossible trio of mountain peaks and survived.

Next morning, reason returned, rain settled in, and ten of us were up for a sound scolding. Together we trudged up the hushed stairs of Haupthaus into Paulus's small study, the sign of something truly important, but at first it didn't seem that important to me, surrounded by my friends, most of us hungover, miming embarrassment and shame. Armin led the "discussion" with his usual emphasis on community, how these uprisings were damaging to the Ecole's way of life, and was this behavior the example we wanted to present to younger students? Were we aware that any future such incident, even one, might lead to expulsion? Yes, the teachers and staff of the Ecole d'Humanité were *serious*, and yes, they expected far more of us. We shuffled on to breakfast. Everyone was stunned and no one was feeling particularly rhapsodic.

Just like that Tobias was lost to me. He half-heartedly waved across the dining hall but headed off in the opposite direction. I heard him mutter to someone: "*Zeit, um meine Unterhose zu wechseln.*" Time to change my underpants. That's what I was, a boy's dirty underwear. My mouth was cottony and sour. Sociologists have suggested that adolescents have trouble reading the emotional signals of others, but that was not *my* problem. This message was loud and clear. I instantly regretted throwing away my favorite flannel shirt.

After breakfast, Tobias peeled off with his usual friends as we all set about our chores, which today included removing hundreds of broken branches, sweeping of wayward trash, and repairing of skewed shutters. We shuffled into classrooms and began our studies. Each hour spent in the steady progress toward evening was relief. The wind tucked in its gigantic tail and died on its way to the next canton. I'd been blown apart in a brief, hallucinatory, amorous consummation and now returned to the fold, pressed into place like fabric, with weight and impeccable creases. It hurt like the body hurts after unusual exercise or a sudden pitch down a ravine.

Forty years later, I watched Tobias on YouTube, baffling and amazing both young and old. When his parents retired, he'd taken over *Looslis Puppentheater* and occasionally appeared as the magician Buccini, chatting up audiences on two continents. Tonight, he demonstrated the vanishing silk trick: he plucked it from nowhere, waved it about, stuffed it lustily into his fist, then threw it to the wind with a barely perceptible flick of his hand.

Oh, I knew that trick.

Snapshots

▲▲▲ 9:20 a.m.

Next door, an engine sputters and dies in a small backyard. Half is patio and half lawn. Mixed in with the grass are hundreds of foot-high white asters with pink stamens that sway prettily. I imagined the flowers were intentional till morning broke and the owner fired up her lawnmower, which is now humming smoothly. She's made up her mind and proceeds in long, even stripes, back and forth. But, and this is odd, she pauses for a few minutes after exactly two steps. So it goes: step mow, step mow, stop, step mow, step mow, stop, while the machine masticates a square meter and whisks the trimmings into the attached bag. She is curiously considerate of her machine, the precise opposite of an adolescent across the street who, at his father's repeated requests, mows his lawn as quickly as possible. He slams around fence posts, weaves back and forth, charges carelessly over stones and twigs. If the mower chokes, the kid gets to finish early. Nothing to be done. Take the rest of the afternoon off.

▲▲▲ 12:41 p.m.

The train windows of my adolescence slid open to let in that cold-streaming mountain air. Now they are sealed, the compartments hot and airless. No need for that woman across the aisle to rise, lurch over my legs and backpack to close the window. No need for the conductor to issue his crisp warning: "*Bitte öffnen Sie nicht die Fenster, vor allem in Tunneln.*" In all other matters not resolved by design, there's a right and a wrong way, and not much between. Commit a cultural faux pas and prepare to be called on it. No bicycling on the sidewalk, even for a second. Clean up that *Apfelsaft*. You spilled it. The cadence will be accusative; you're guilty, guilty, guilty. Indeed, there's some *defect* in your character.

It takes some nerve to insist that a stranger correct a mistake—pick up her trash or move her car to a legal parking spot. You are interfering with an individual's freedom, though many Swiss citizens feel they should intervene for society's sake. There's even a word for it: *Zivilcourage*, from the Latin *civilis*, meaning "civilian," or "acceptable," and the French *courage*. Zivilcourage is especially important where young people are concerned. The Swiss view the rearing of children as society's task, along with parents of course. Passersby will admire babies, prattle with toddlers, and also tell them off when necessary. However, if the scolding goes on too long, it's appropriate to come back: Listen, I know that you are not happy with what just happened, but I'm a fine person, and you can talk to me in a different tone of voice. And they might back right down. Yeah.

▲▲▲ 9:45 a.m.

Church bells crash through the Haslital. They toll chaotically for a full quarter hour, announcing the commencement of St. Michael's Sunday morning worship. The sound is joyous and oddly comic, but only a handful of people walk up from the village and file into the church. Surprising, considering the sonic enthusiasm. We count just two or three pairs of *Alten*, gray-haired and slow of pace.

There's a less embarrassing turnout inside. Seated toward the front of more than forty pews is a large family of well-dressed locals, including two pairs of girl twins, one set in their early teens, the other close to thirty, and all four just beautiful. Turns out this will be a special service. A baptism! The candidate is a two-year-old boy (still) sucking on a pacifier, attached string dangling well below his knees. He wanders about and women attempt unsuccessfully to reel him in, their arms extending along his path like lappets. The German word for "organ" is *orgel*. Absolutely dreadful, not unlike the English "organ," with its intimations of dark, slimy interior body parts. *Die Organistin* adjusts her rearview mirror. The congregation quiets. A violinist raises her bow, and an elegiac duet begins, the first of three movements.

Reform Swiss Evangelical is the chosen denomination here and what does that mean exactly? We recognize the structure: Collect, three readings, two from the *Paulusbriefe*. Then, baptism with a guest minister in a wool suit, who needs the deacon's help attaching his microphone. The occasion warrants a little fun and so appears an enormous, rainbow-colored pinwheel on a stick too long to be practical or safe, carried from the back of the church to Christoph, the baptizee. He reaches, squirms in his mother's arms. The stick careens by her face not to mention her husband's close-set eyes, and she blushes pink from the effort to keep him still. While the minister chugs along, entreating the godparents and also the congregation (all thirty of us) to keep watch over this child's Christian upbringing as God watches over us, the candidate slips from his mother's grasp and parades around the font, up and down the steps, dangling his mother's digital camera. At last he's lifted by the minister like a newborn and tipped into the font. The boy stills. Time slows down for three lovely minutes and we observe the holy water trickle from its ceramic pitcher over the child's bare scalp, falling with a burble like a silver charm bracelet into the basin. Christoph is dried, anointed, and sealed with consecrated oil. A faint cross remains, glistening on his forehead. No one could watch this scene and not be moved, whatever language, whatever religion.

But this is Reform Swiss Evangelical and we notice there is no sharing of the peace; no group amen following the prayers, not even the Lord's Prayer, which in Hochdeutsch sounds unexpectedly graceful; no crossing of the body index finger to forehead, shoulders, belly, and heart. No crosses anywhere, actually, except in one stained glass window, weighing on Jesus's back. The body of our Lord is distributed—real bread, meaty and freshly baked. But the blood is mere grape juice, served in individual stoneware shot glasses from a silver tray, perhaps to ensure no mix of congregational saliva, despite the blood's putative purity and uplifting effects.

And today, perhaps because it's a special service, no welcoming of newcomers, either. That would be the Americans, awkwardly shuffling to the back of the church. As a rule, these Swiss are slow to make contact with strangers, yet they are often more tolerant. Same-sex marriage, for example, is legal. *Those two men shopping, gardening, living together in that little house up the alley? Fine people. Not bothering me. Why should I have anything to say about it? Not really my business.* On the other hand, come Sunday and a street fair with music and grilled sausages, those two men may not be invited over to your picnic table, though there's obviously room and no place else to sit. Not sure what to do with a couple composed of two men.

▲▲▲ 5:26 p.m.

All over the world, in every geographic area, there are outsiders—people who, for one reason or another, don't fit. In Meiringen, gateway to three mountain passes (Grimsel, Susten, Brünig), there's a small convenience store called Avec, adjacent to the train station. It offers most necessities at slightly higher prices than markets like Migros or coop, though coffee and pastries are cheap. Four small tables and several aluminum chairs are positioned close to the sliding glass door. From here we gaze on the back side of an apartment building, pink with maroon trim, small balcony at the third level with a man in rumpled T-shirt and swim trunks, his feet planted on the railing. Other elements include the PostBus parking lot, where two large tourist buses are idling. Yes, there's a hulking mountain ridge behind all this, but the near view is 90 percent concrete. Between the cigarette smoke and bus fumes, it's hard to breathe. That doesn't deter a small cluster of Portuguese, red-tan from toiling in the sun, streaming both smoke and rippling sentences. They are among the many "guest workers," Switzerland depends on—paid (poorly) to pick up the garbage, wash the dishes, change the sheets, maintain the streets. Their jests and squabbling are a high-speed wake compared to the bouncy splashes of the two Swiss Germans, sitting to their right—one scary skinny, the other overweight, both with stringy hair and fading tattoos. In between Swiss and Portuguese is the spot where my husband, a recovering alcoholic, chooses to write. "My tribe," he calls them.

We think of the United States as the land of freedom, yet law and litigation dissuade many citizens from following their bliss. You're not supposed to drive a car without a seatbelt. You cannot drop out of the sky from a biplane and land in just anyone's backyard. In some ways, the Swiss have a more relaxed attitude about individual rights. You *can* jump into the Rhein in Basel, where enormous barges traffic. You can parasail—solo, if you want—and risk slamming into mountain faces. It's legal to commit suicide in order to escape a slow cumbersome death, and if you wish to be present with your partner during this tragic act, that's OK too. A Brit might be tried as accessory to murder.

Responsible autonomy. Self-reliance that also behaves well. This is the goal.

▲▲▲ 10:36 a.m.

The funicular to the Grandhotel Giessbach takes two men to run, both well into their sixties, both smartly uniformed in blue and white, red caps and shoulder satchels. They interact with passengers, many of them guests of the hotel, others just visitors arriving to soak in old world luxury without contending with new world prices. A passenger is chatting them up in mellifluous, jaunty Swiss German. They nod and chortle and turn politely for a few minutes as if to scoop me up into the conversation. I listen for several minutes until I have to tell them, "*Es tut mir leid, aber ich habe fast nichts verstanden*" (I'm sorry but I hardly understood anything), which sends them over the roof with hilarity. I fork over my ten SF note. They are retired men, clearly enjoying their minimal duties, pleased as punch in each other's company.

However, as the minute hand on the oversized clock clicks toward eleven, they immediately cut off the talk and get down to business. One operates the sliding hatches, locking passengers into their open-aired, shellacked-benched compartments. The other walks to the front of the train, flips open the lid of a long metal box to reveal the controls, which are pretty straightforward: red for stop, yellow for slow, green for proceed. The train inches up the steep track, loops outward at a midway point to allow its downhill twin, loaded with departing guests, to pass safely on its sea-bent route. This has all been carefully considered: a seven-minute descent followed by a six-minute wait at the dock as the steamboat *Lötschland* arrives punctually at 12:11. After loading, there's a ten-minute, wind-tickled ride across the deep waters of Brienz to the rail station, where passengers are allotted eight minutes to cross the tracks, including a three-minute wait at the train crossing as the barriers come down. Watch a tourist stamp her foot, worrying what anyone would worry before acquainted with reliable Swiss transportation. As the barriers begin to rise, the woman and a man duck underneath and run to catch the train, which doesn't depart till 12:32. Actually, folks, there's time to kill.

Much of Swiss culture can be tidily traced to the landscape—mountains isolating life for centuries and centuries. The Alps are formidable, winters often extreme with much precipitation. If you are to raise cattle and children and not starve, you have to prepare, prepare, prepare in advance. Stock your cellar with root vegetables from the garden, scythe the grass a certain number of times a season so your store of hay allows the animals to survive. You must approach your tasks with a well-reasoned, organized mind.

▲▲▲ 8:35 a.m.

To finesse and penetrate the Swiss wall of *ordentlich*, it's useful to know they like to be asked for help. Rather than jump right in with your wish for directions or the platform number for a Schnellzug or a new half-price tourist card, pose the question this way: "Hello, may I ask you something? I have a problem. I lost my *Halb-Preis Karte*. Can you suggest what I might do?"

Heading toward Bern, we drive our miniature rental into a gas station to fill up the tank. There's no cap, just a valve that will accept only the correct fuel. I pull out my credit card and face the pump, dumbfounded. Where's the slide in? Keypad? I'm forced to enter the

minimart to ask how I'm expected to pay. The cashier is momentarily flummoxed. Luckily, a dark-haired young man, waiting with pastry
and espresso, leaves the queue to show me the particulars: "Use this
nozzle, not that. Pay afterward at the register."

"You mean they trust me? What if I drive off?"

"You won't," he says.

A Mountain Feeling

> Entire mountains and fortresses of cloud seem almost indolent, like swans
> swimming along or women being disposed to smile or to move.
> —ROBERT WALSER

Three of the highest peaks in Switzerland—the Finsteraarhorn,
Jungfrau, and Mönch—sit in Canton Bern, but none of these are visible from the village of Goldern. What you *can* see, what dominates the
horizon magnificently like Glinda the Good Witch dressed in white
chiffon and blue tulle, are the Wetterhorn, Mittelhorn, and Rosenhorn,
three pinnacles forming the Wetterhorn massif. They are, respectively,
12,113, 12,152, and 12,103 feet of rock and timber, snow and ice. Like
Glinda, they're in the prime of their lives, young enough to startle with
their looks, timeless in their mystery and clout.

Mountains are symbols of the breast and phallus and home to Greek
deities. Zeus rumbled and hurled lightning from Mount Olympus.
God routinely required prophets to meet Him on high. During the
terrible flood, Noah's ark tied up at Ararat (16,854 feet), Armenia's
Mount Olympus. Young mountains are Beethoven mountains: thun-
derous, heroic, daunting in their extraordinary gorgeousness, their high
broad foreheads jutting outward. They cut through the clouds with ser-
rated edges, vertiginous precipices, and sudden avalanches. Old mountains, on the other hand, have been worn down by time and erosion;
their profiles are smooth and gentle. The Appalachians were born 480
million years ago. It's hard to imagine, but perhaps the Green, White,
Smoky, and Shenandoah peaks once resembled the Alps themselves.

A mountain, rather like a person, ages into moderation; its history is a leveling of extremes.

Spread a tablecloth out on a well-polished wood table, then push it gently from one side, and you will create a bunching effect. This is how the Alps were formed roughly 300 million years ago. Tectonic plates rubbed together, their edges crumbled, forcing gigantic folds upward (anticlines) and downward (synclines). These plates may be "local" or originate in far away places. For instance, the Matterhorn consists of a basement nappe structure (rock sheet) from continental Europe. Above are layers of Tethyan marine sediment—particles of crushed shell, pulverized skeletons of coral and mollusk from the enormous shallow sea that once stretched from Europe to central Asia. Finally, at the tip are gneisses from the African tectonic plate. The best place to observe this lateral compression is directly in front of a sheer rock face. Amazing—Africa traveled all this way and wound up as *the* classic emblem of Switzerland.

For many centuries, there wasn't much to encourage actual exploration among the loftiest Swiss peaks: little arable land or game, intense

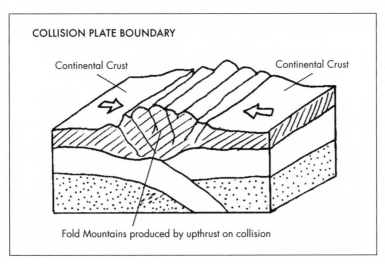

COLLISION PLATE BOUNDARY

Continental Crust

Continental Crust

Fold Mountains produced by upthrust on collision

Mountain folds.

cold, and precarious footing. Thus, they inspired some pretty wild ideas. Shaggy-furred creatures resided among the rocks and glaciers and walked upright like men. Two-headed dragons crouched inside caves, poised to incinerate climbers if they dared approach.

In 1854, British explorer Alfred Wills launched the golden age of alpinism by scaling the Wetterhorn. He claimed to be the first, though in reality, Swiss climbers Johann Jaun and Melchior Bannholzer laid down first tracks a decade earlier. Wills got credit because he published a detailed account in his book, *Wanderings among the High Alps*, a fascinating and often humorous record of several expeditions.

He did not travel solo on his ambitious trek. He engaged four Swiss guides, a porter, and mounds of equipment to ensure the journey would be as comfortable as possible. As he prepared to depart from the small Grindelwald hotel, its innkeeper blurted out: "Try to return, all of you. Alive." Then he scuttled quickly back inside. Fortunately Wills was prudent in his first choice of escorts—Ulrich Lauener, renowned in the Oberland, whom Wills describes as "straight as an arrow, more than six feet tall, spare, muscular, and active, health and vigour glowing in his open and manly countenance, his clear blue eye sparkling with vivacity and good temper, a slight dash of rough and careless swagger in his attitude and manner . . . the genius of the place." Lauener was someone to trust. To demonstrate, he led the way with a ten-foot wrought-iron pole and flag strapped to his back. He would plant it on the summit.

For hours the men scrambled over moraine, clear cold streams, crags ascending at right angles, and glaciers winding down from the mountaintop "bathed in a flood of purple." They spent their first night in a cave formed by two enormous boulders leaning against each other. Hunters had been here before them; a thick coat of damp hay covered the floor. Wills complained "there was no boiled cream or chicken this time"; they had to make do with black coffee, cold veal, and a hunk of stale bread. They passed an uncomfortable night on frigid stones seasoned with a strong smell of mold and set out the next morning at 4:30.

Their chief concern after they successfully traversed one glacier was debris, which Wills called "nervous work." As he wrote:

The substratum appeared to be a schistaceous gneiss, very friable and much disintegrated by the weather; so that every particle had to be tried, before it was safe to trust hand or foot to it. It was extremely steep; very often, the ledges which gave us foot-hold were but an inch or two wide, and throughout, it was a marvel to me that rocks which, from a short distance off, looked such absolute precipices could be climbed at all.

The view came and went as they zigzagged up the final stretch. At one point a pair of peasants, one with a young fir tree on his back, passed Wills's party while they were having lunch. "A great shouting now took place between the two parties, the result of which was, that the piratical adventurers promised to wait for us on the rocks above." Offered slices of chocolate cake, they joined the group, taking up the rear.

As they neared the top, the party was met with a serious obstacle, an overhanging crest of ice and snow. The slope leading up began at an angle of forty-five degrees and steepened to nearly seventy. Lauener again took the lead and hammered into the ice swinging his right arm backward as far as he dared. The ice gave way, crashing down, grazing the waiting climbers. He gave an exalted cry, "*Ich schaue den blauen Himmel!*" (I look upon the blue sky!) The glorious summit lay just beyond. Wills scooted along the last ridge in a sitting position, till he felt confident enough to stand upright. The path was only four inches wide, with sheer drops on either side. Finally, they took in the 360-degree panorama:

> To the east and south lay a boundless sea of mighty peaks, stretching
> from the great Ortler Spitz, and his mighty companions of the Tyrol, in
> the solemn distance, past the fine group of the Monte Leone, the many
> summits of Monte Rosa, and the sharp peak of the Weisshorn, towards
> the western extremity of the Pennine chain. Mont Blanc was hidden
> behind the mountains of the Oberland, whose stupendous masses
> looked but a stone's throw from us . . . at the foot of which tortuous
> mountain torrents and glacier streams glittered like silver threads. The
> immediate group of the Oberland presented a scene of indescribable
> sublimity . . . and then came the wedge-like form of the Eigher, rising

in a thin slice a thousand feet above the height on which we stood. This mountain, too steep to allow more than a thin and broken coating of snow to rest upon its northern side, presents from this point of view, a peculiarly majestic and imposing appearance.... It seemed as if anything let slip from the top would slide many thousands of feet before it met with any obstacle to divert it. After all, however, the most interesting part of the view lay nearer to us. It was impossible long to turn the eye from the fearful slope at the top of which we stood. For twenty or thirty yards below us, the glacier curved away steeper and steeper ... nothing else broke the terrific void ... and made our hearts beat quicker with a solemn and strange emotion.

They did not bother to use telescopes, as "we did not wish to ruin any chance of weakening the steadiness of the eye." The guides busied themselves by hammering the flagpole six feet into the ice. When the men finished, they attached the flag itself, a sheet of iron three feet wide and four feet long that swung back and forth on its hinges. Suddenly, they noticed another flag perched at the end of the ridge, a short distance below. These mountaineers had *almost* made it but were averted by the ice crest. In Wills's estimation, he and his climbers remained the very first to reach the summit. The party spent a mere twenty minutes admiring the view. Eager to arrive home at the predicted hour, even earlier perhaps, they turned around. If nothing else, mountaineers like to be engaged in mountaineering whether up or down.

On clear winter mornings, we estimate time by the sun's progress over snow-capped peaks, through steep pastures, down gravel paths and roads. Sometimes, ice sizzles in its melting, hurried along by tires and boot prints. This light is unlike that in any prairie, plateau, or field—crystal sharp and intense, the altitude enhancing focus and refraction. Every misplaced hair or pimple or hanging thread is spot lit—too much exposure for the adolescent, who sinks into her shirt all the way up to her nose.

As the sun sets, the Engelhörner morph into prehistoric mode. The drop in temperature is dramatic, always unsettling. Sweaters are whipped off their hangers and jackets zipped up to the chin. We've all heard the expressions: *the shadow knows, a shadow passed over her face.* But it's more of an enveloping, a set of rough wings closing around us. I've watched as they snuff out vast swaths of stars and cast shadows in the weak light of the moon. Their silhouettes are hard to discern, but peer down into the valley and you may catch sight of one bisecting a rooftop with a wedge of deeper black, ragged as lump charcoal.

In all the sci-fi movies I've seen, enemy starships float like untethered rock masses, sinister and rumbling. Perhaps the Alps are more benign—sleepy giants who may or may not shuffle around in gigantic snowshoes—nocturnal, but made of earth. They travel when no one is looking. Perhaps their pajamas are stitched from tree bark and lichen. Perhaps their footfalls explain the occasional seismic shudders we felt in bed. I tried to imitate their speech, but the thin magnetic hum was furtive. A dog whistle doesn't come close.

Here is an old super-eight movie of three girls charging up a hill at full speed, racing to see who will first reach the top. The slope is steep and all three collapse halfway up with fatigue, panting and laughing. Soon they take in the scene from above. *This will be great fun; this part is easy.* Holding hands they begin to run and soon their legs are unable to keep up with gravity's pull. They pitch forward, somersault, and tumble down the grass. The children have not figured out how to adjust their bodies to the terrain. It's no longer amusing—insanely violent, in fact. A grounds man watches from below, thinking, *My god they will break their skinny little necks.* His shouts of concern evaporate. The hill wins this race. The children lose. And learn.

Every fall, classes were dismissed for a three-day hike. Students were divided into groups according to their ability and adults led the way, overseeing routes, provisions, and packing of rucksacks. We trained with the lesser hills, like Bidmi just above the school, graduating to Käserstatt, Hochmoor, Schwarzhorn, and finally a six-day *Wanderung* in the spring that took us further and higher. In the beginning, I suffered. I wheezed and stumbled and protested. It was a severe kind of humiliation, clumsiness made worse by teachers who inevitably uttered little nips of militaristic encouragement along the way. They knew we trod on the back of an enormous, intractable animal. Trains and buses and chairlifts make you forget that.

The areas we avoided were naked veinlike stripes running from mountaintop to pasture below, splitting forests like the part in a girl's hair. These inclines were fast-moving thoroughfares for rock and runoff—so steep no foot, claw, or seed could possibly stick. At the base might be a talus heap or thirty-foot snow pyramid, which K.C. and his Ecole Familie came upon one year during a spring hike through the Urbach valley. Before anyone thought to warn them, K.C. and two friends scrambled up and fake-slalomed downhill in their boots. The snow was pure corn, sloppy and wet; their boots and socks soaked through; and the adults beckoned from the sidelines, but the boys didn't care. Later, as everyone packed up their picnic and headed home through the valley, they heard a rolling boom and, glancing back, saw an avalanche shoot over the lip of a high cliff and drop roughly three hundred feet before landing in the Urbach with a mythical splash of gray-green wings. It was a relatively close call and K.C.'s first encounter with the indisputable forces governing this valley for thousands of years.

Whether walking up or down, I soon learned to keep my vision narrowed to a three or four foot semicircle in front of me. Everything I cared about came down to these humpbacked roots and slivers of limestone crumbled to dust, the miniature Matterhorns that dug into my boot soles. A trail offered so many possibilities: right or left, dozens of obstacles, hazards of water mixed with loam on layers of shale. The mountain was my "absorbing errand," as Henry James put it in his famous quote: "True happiness, we are told, consists in getting out of one's self; but the point is not only to get out—you must stay out; and to stay out you must have some absorbing errand." If downhill, I moved wide and low like the legs of a lunar landing module. If uphill, I slowed till my breath was in line with the grade. For once I didn't care if the rest of my group bulldogged ahead or lagged behind. No time for conversation in any case, no wind for a sentence. A little soldiering song stuck in my head. Wordless, for the mountain had my complete attention. Once I got a rhythm going, this kind of "companionship" made me unspeakably happy.

And the views, no matter where we hiked, were stunning—brand-new considerations of a familiar peak or a top-down perspective on the valley, both silence-making and blood-stilling. Rivers below were misted over. It seemed we could ride a distant glacier (if only we had the right-sized sled), glide over crevices as if they were undulating folds in a baby-blue blanket. Red-roofed chalets shrank to Monopoly pieces, their inhabitants unseen. Above, the sky stretched as far as peripheral and my twenty-seventy vision would allow. Was it really that clear, an expanse I could get lost or be found in?

Even if we didn't subscribe to God, heaven, or hell, we were palpably close to the celestial. Percy Bysshe Shelley while vacationing in the Chamonix Valley enthused in his travel journal:

> The snowy Alps are a hundred miles distant, but reach so high in the heavens, that they look like those accumulated clouds of dazzling white that arrange themselves on the horizon during summer. Their immensity staggers the imagination, and so far surpasses all conception, that it requires an effort of the understanding to believe that they indeed form a part of the earth.

Upon arrival, he had signed his hotel registry "Atheos." But after he took a good look around he remarked: "Who would be, who could be an atheist in this valley of wonders?" Indeed, in their writings early church fathers saw the material world as the constant image of the spirit world. Among the juniper trees and snow-capped mountains of Lebanon they discerned the thoughts of God. Can we imagine what they would have seen in the Alps?

Gorgeous, stunning, beautiful, absolute, sublime, glorious, mighty, boundless, stupendous, majestic, imposing, spectacular, fearful. Just some of the many overused adjectives we use to describe the indescribable quality of mountains, including "indescribable." Even the best writers, past and present, have struggled to offer more than this. For me, the word "sublime" stood out for its implied polarity—that terror could be tempered with awe, and pain coexist with pleasure, for wasn't I swinging wildly between these points as thousands of others had done before me? Think of Yeats's "tragic joy" or Kant's "the noble, the splendid, and the terrifying."

But perhaps the precise modifier was not the point. In any case, I was faced with a phenomenon far beyond my small history, impossible to grasp especially at my age. I certainly could not duplicate it for later cherishing, though I snapped a pathetic photo here and there with my Kodak Instamatic. The photograph we take of a looming mountain peak is likely to disappoint, revealing a midget where we would expect to find a giant. Baby Rothorn. Slightly taller miniature Schreckhorn. Too much was left out of the frame, just as my memory failed to register the physical sensations of height—chest fullness and a spinning brain.

It is possible when a person effuses *I love you, I love you, I love you so much*, she is begging instead to be forgiven, to be reassured, to be loved back. A mountain, a waterfall, a river, a stream, a pasture can never love you back. And therein lay some comfort. I didn't have to fold this feeling in, translate, or record. The experience could exist outside and beyond me. I needn't carry it home like some souvenir to wave in front of my friends.

After that, I didn't really know what to do with the view except say *wow*, admire it for a respectable amount of time, and like Alfred Wills, simply turn around. The tangible sensation of foot on stone, leaping when it was safe, the warming air, pine-needle laden forest floor, bare twigs etching calves and thighs, bug bites, bird droppings, sunburn, all these things awaited. It didn't matter if my gait was graceful or gawky as long as I established that steady intimacy with the trail. If nothing else, hikers like to be engaged in hiking, whether up or down.

▲▲▲

I live in a corner of the world where the human mark on native terrain is obvious and disturbing. Residential areas moved eastward from the city, gathering momentum in the early 2000s, then slowing, thanks to a sustained housing crisis. In one recent newspaper photo, a developer holds a shovel, posing like Edmund Hillary before two hundred acres of stripped forest—naked clay and tree stumps, not a tendril of green remaining. Oh, he'll be reseeding, replanting, rearranging to make this place homey, an asset to the community. But for now, the effect is apocalyptic. With sod and maples in place, the panorama of Homearamas will be a snore at best.

At first I assumed that Switzerland's landscape was God-patterned and virginal. Emerald green pastures adjoined coniferous forests that lay across the highlands like mink stoles. Riverbanks and lake beaches were trim and free of clutter. Anywhere I hiked, no matter the elevation, the scenery was aesthetically lovely. The mountains, of course, formed a natural frame, and wasn't all of this thousands of years old, well beyond our meddling?

Not exactly. Once I took a walk along a cliff-side *Strasse* and, shifting my gaze from macro to micro, noticed a bolt in the rock. Then, a few more bolts, some with hinges. More hinges, latches, and behold—a large symmetrical, distinctly dome-shaped indentation. Hardly natural or even the remains of an old road sign. Indeed, the rock in this particular spot didn't feel like rock either, though it was certainly convincing.

Turns out, hollowed-out sections of the Bernese Alps, like many other mountain ranges in Switzerland, shelter a vast supply of military munitions. In *La Place de la Concorde Suisse*, John McPhee tells an engrossing story of the Swiss Army, which at the time his book appeared numbered more than 650,000, pretty impressive for a neutral country. Reform has brought that number down, but the Swiss principle of defense remains: *Like a porcupine, you roll up into a ball and brandish your quills.* Every tunnel near neighboring countries is wired to collapse shut with a few strategically placed explosives. Talus slopes can be similarly coaxed to fall over highways. Quaint little mountain huts and cow barns sit atop basements full of guns. Says one of McPhee's informants: "Switzerland does not have an army. Switzerland *is* an army."

There's a military landing strip in Meiringen that resembles at most a slice of marooned parking lot. I wouldn't have noticed if the occasional fighter jet hadn't careened into the picture. Only a specially trained pilot can put down jets in valleys this narrow. They display no contrails. They drag the roar of their engines several seconds behind. But no one I knew ever asked why aircraft flew in this valley so far from the nerve centers of war. Why full-uniformed soldiers were drinking beer from chilled glasses at the local *Gasthaus*. Sunday was target practice in pastures near our school. We were aware of a dim popping sound throughout the day and, at breakfast, the usual announcements were slightly stepped up: *Die Weiden* (fields) were off limits today, for the soldiers were serious and used real ammunition.

Otherwise, the small-town Swiss appeared perfectly in sync with their surroundings. Oh, happy valleys, tucked into their high-walled beds! Ancient churches that tolled the hours and still offered services! Farmers with their huge wooden rakes and piles of newly mown hay! Down from the highlands came the cows, up they clattered in the spring, driven by boys along twisting narrow roads. Here a bright red gondola or funicular clicking in and out of the station. The overall touch was timelessness, containment. God was a sunny, sound-minded painter who ignored gray areas and shading. Divisions of pasture and creek were sharp and clean as if an invisible giant with a weed-whacker kept on top of it for centuries. Where were the edge species, ecotones of snarled vines and trash trees so common in the United States? Maybe they just didn't exist here.

In fact, nearly every blade of grass I saw in this splendid countryside was intentional and managed by agronomists who strategized the ratio of pasture to forest, field to stream. As McPhee pointed out: "While making their artifacts everywhere attractive, the Swiss have not embarrassed their terrain." Much of Swiss agriculture, especially the dairy industry, couldn't survive without government support. Its continued existence is key to tourism and the country's cultural identity. Even fencing is subsidized and the natives are serious about their fences, be they wood or wire. No one is allowed to cut down trees without a permit. If a tenant farmer should fail to keep up his allotted acres, the authorities are notified. I can't recall any plastic bottles, cigarette butts, burned-out matches feathering roadsides or heaped around bus stops. I hike toward Käserstatt, where workers are "constructing" a mountain moor. Those huge piles of manure sit on cement slabs outside barns, many of them close to the road, but they are squared off and contained as much as possible with two-by-fours. Their scent is part of the scenery.

In their use of land, the Swiss are judicious and respectful. Still, as the country's population grows and tourism expands, some of Switzerland's natural resources are under threat. Farming, a mainstay during the Middle Ages, is still important in the twenty-first century and herbicides, insecticides, fungicides, and other agrochemicals have leeched into the soil. The Swiss Plateau in particular is suffering a loss of biodiversity as some natural habitats are disturbed. There are currently sixty-eight species on the endangered species list. To help offset this, roughly 29 percent of the countryside was designated protected natural area.

Swiss farmers can qualify for payment if they set aside at least 7 percent of their land for ECAs, or ecological compensation areas. But little was known about how the public might react to these changes, and such knowledge is particularly important in tourist destinations and recreational areas. Thus, in 2010, a survey was sent out to 202 Swiss residents asking for preferences in the "look" of a landscape. The survey contained manipulated photographs of areas in the Eastern Central Alps. Multiple scenarios were put forward. One example: pasture with species-rich grasslands in the foreground at 100 percent, 50 percent, and 0 percent.

Turned out, elderly citizens didn't mind seeing acres of wheat, barley, or other crops; they rather liked it since it hearkened back to a landscape they remembered and thought of as typically Swiss. But most everyone else preferred the species-rich grasslands with locally adapted trees and hedges and found the arable land "boring," though "productive." The survey determined that reserving grasslands for species diversity could have a positive effect on tourism.

Preserving the natural environment is a modern priority, especially among young people. It's also worth noting that Switzerland hosts the world's largest, and oldest, global environmental organization,

"Middle Ground." These manipulated photographs show species-rich grasslands in the foreground at 0 percent, 50 percent, and 100 percent.

the International Union for Conservation of Nature, established near Geneva. In this way, the Swiss have inched closer to the American environmentalist view, which values a landscape in its purest and most expansive form. Wilderness is second only to the divine, a kind of Eden. Visitors to the great parks of the West are just that—*visitors*—and we're instructed to stay on the trail, to leave the flowers and animals alone, for the land belongs to them.

Either way—through farming, forestry, or native planting—much of Switzerland's landscape evolved as a distinct result of human, even political, action. The Swiss approach to land manipulation is perhaps less objectionable because the results are so tasteful. As McPhee noted, Switzerland is one of the most magnificent gardens in Europe.

▲▲▲

Fifty yards below the Wetterhorn summit, Alfred Wills pulled out a bottle of brandy and, mixing it with a bit of snow, drank to the health of the mountain. He meant to toast on the actual summit but the party's footing had been far too shaky for balancing glasses and a bottle made slippery by sweat and snow. They wisely decided that heading back up for this purpose would be frivolous and unsafe.

Refreshed, they continued in their descent, keeping up a swift pace, though return trips are often the most dangerous part of an expedition. There were many difficulties, including a treacherous ridge, the narrow goat-track of the Enge, and sections of gneiss soaked by a recent rain. When they reached the glacier, they found

> a grand place for a glissade. There was but one crevasse of any consequence, some distance below, and I marked a wide bridge of snow and ice in the middle, which made it perfectly safe in that direction. Accordingly, I made for a point in the glacier above this bridge, and having gained it, I took a little run, planted my alpenstock behind me, and went sliding down at railroad pace. Lauener was behind, and never having been out with me before, was not assured that I knew what I was about, and how to direct my course towards the point where the crevasse was safe. Accordingly he set off after me with a shout of

"Halte! Halte!" and overtaking me, seized me by the arm to stop me. The consequence was, that we both rolled over together, and had the greatest difficulty in stopping ourselves. My hand, grasping my alpenstock, got ground between his heavy body and the hard, granulated snow; the skin was taken off all the knuckles; but fortunately we succeeded in checking our descent, with no worse result.

After his ride, Wills had time to observe the surrounding vegetation, what little there was. He found only *Campanula cenisia* above the glacier, small starbursts of lavender wedged between loose sections of rock. Further down, he found three species of blue gentian (*acaulis, verna,* and *nivalis*) ranging in color from pale pink to royal blue. A large flock of sheep joined the team just as they came to the *mauvais pas*—a slab of rock with terrible footing. Once they reached their provisions, they again indulged in celebratory glasses of chilled red wine. Finally, just an hour from their destination, Wills was greeted on the path by his wife and a brisk salute of guns in honor of his arrival. She remounted her mule and fell in behind her husband as they headed to Grindelwald, where a small parade gathered. The descent had taken a mere six hours.

Wills wraps up his account of the Wetterhorn excursion with a summary of expenses, an analysis of the weather, and a description of his blotched, purple face, which suffered considerably in the high sun and altitude. He writes that the guides, locals, and pretty much everyone else were duly impressed with his accomplishment. One peasant referred to him as *Der Wetterhörner Herr.* Auguste Balmat and Auguste Simond Sampson added to the ovation, calling the ascent of Mont Blanc a bagatelle in comparison with the Wetterhorn. Wills's overall tone is ebullient, satisfied, but gracious, as he notes how he never would have succeeded were it not for the assistance of his Swiss guides, especially "El Capitan" Ulrich Lauener.

▲▲▲

Today, Switzerland offers generous and reliable guidance as you walk from village to village. Trails are easy to follow: posted with bright

Trail signs at
one rather busy
intersection.

yellow directional signs, indicating how many *Stunden* and *Minuten* to this *Dorf* or that peak.

Technical routes, requiring special equipment, are marked by blue and white stripes across rock faces. There are main roads, narrow secondary roads, gravel trails, and dirt paths in order of width, most of them marked. They wind behind little huts and vacation homes with tiny cars in tiny garages. On hillsides they'll occasionally peter into nothing more than cow paths, ribbons of compressed soil, unevenly pitched, and no thicker than one set of human toes. If you're alone, this can be confusing. Should you push on, or turn back? A stream appears suddenly, sunk two feet into the grass, like liquid avalanche or irrigation ditch gone rogue. These babbles and raspberries create a swirl of negative ions making the climbing easier and more wonderful. Your worry subsides. Many more steps up and deciduous fades to coniferous. The air is downright cold. Here is a bench, rubbed shiny in spots, thoughtfully placed for just one of the many jaw-dropping vistas. And now, pine scrub thins to lichen and foot-worn areas disappear completely over vast stretches of rock. Above, the Englehörner expand—darker, fatter, their wing tips sharp and scary.

We're all too familiar with climbing lingo, the testosterone-fueled illusion that someone can "conquer" or "capture" a summit. A feminine approach might express it differently, as going *into* the mountain, lingering, walking as a way of experiencing or knowing the place. Either way, the mountain will always have the last word. The Alps ascended, scaled, scrambled, and crawled over are still the Alps. No choice but to breathe in their arrogance till you can smell it on your skin. Time to put a sweater on?

Mountains are everywhere—in France, Italy, India, Spain, Afghanistan, Colorado, New Mexico, and Vermont. The Alps sheltered Benedictine and Cistercian monks. They nearly killed Hannibal, along with his army of forty-six thousand men and thirty-seven elephants. They produced bronze for the Celts, gold for the Romans, ore for the steel industry, amethysts for jewelers. They concealed Nazi loot and Swiss munitions. Their glaciers preserved a Neolithic mummy, Ötzi the Iceman, born circa 3300 BCE and discovered in 1991. By their presence, mountains are the enormous proof of our ephemeral lives. They dash minor ambition and ridicule complacency. They pull us up short and force a high level of achievement, a promise of physical duress and spiritual euphoria.

A mountain feeling was planted in my subconscious at fifteen, and it served nicely to counterpoint the practical education I received at slightly lower elevations in manmade houses and huts. To this day, I cannot help but scrutinize photographs, nineteenth-century paintings, and documentaries for massive clusters of rock. These might momentarily fill me with joy, as in those furry, canine numbers in St. Lucia or Hawaii or China. I flip through the literature of climbing, geography textbooks, random first-person narratives for the mere mention of the word, though it may be couched in simile and have little to do with echt granite or limestone. I've even found myself, like Richard Dreyfuss, slicing a butter knife through a hunk of whipped cream, sculpting the Eiger on one side, the Jungfrau on the other, and the ridgeline between like a crisp Oxford shirtsleeve. This isn't simple curiosity or lust for adventure. This is craving, madness, stronger than ever as time and distance separate me from the real thing. The lack increases my attachment, as if a place can become more desirable when playing hard to get. Dear mountains, you are more absent for being so present in my mind.

Now in the horizontal Midwest, I sit in a city coffee shop with acceptable windows and squint till summer trees ringing the parking lot are sufficiently smudged into an uneven chain of peaks. I stop whatever I'm doing and with my finger in midair trace the Mittelhorn's formidable profile, so much scarier than a Dow Jones plunge or ECG leap. Asleep, it's enough to focus on an imagined horizon, dream-eyes open and flaring. I draw myself up, muster my subconscious powers, point them like a Bond-movie laser, and behold, behold, I can feel it: the mountain appears.

Bites ⋀⋀⋀ Meringue

I tell myself meringue is dessert without guilt because it's only egg whites, because the energy of the whipper passes along to you at no extra charge, because it sits on a plate like a snow-capped bluff, then sinks into your tongue faster than a sliver of ice. You are eating molecules of oxygen strung together with Glinda dust.

Long ago in a valley called Hasli, a local chef concocted a flourless cookie from cinnamon, nuts, sugar, and egg yolks. What to do with the whites? Why not sweeten and fluff them up, bake till crispy, and serve with light cream? Emperor Napoleon was the baker's honored guest, and so very impressed, he named the dessert "meringue" after the Swiss village of Meiringen.

There are less enchanting stories of origin, but who cares? With its frothy peaks brushed with gold, meringue is a miniature temple, begging exploration. Jab it lightly with your dessert fork and one face crumbles, revealing a secret, hallowed room. Sometimes the truth can be found inside a mountain, like Swiss fighter jets lined up for the love of country.

The Accident

In 1954, MGM released a musical film called *Seven Brides for Seven Brothers*. In one scene, seven mountain men ride into the valley homestead of seven beautiful sisters. It's winter and they must pass through a gulch, flanked on both sides by towering snowy cliffs with looming overhangs. They desperately want to marry these women and, given enough time, could easily convince the lot of them. As they clear the gorge, the brothers draw their pistols, briefly swivel their horses about, and fire into the air. The noise, we're led to believe, sets off an enormous avalanche that thunders into the gulch, making it impassable, at least until spring. When they alight on the girls' porch, the brothers are in *aw shucks* mode: "Guess we'll have to stay the winter." By spring each brother has miraculously found his mate and all celebrate with a joyful communal wedding.

The film, of course, is pure romantic fantasy, not the least because it's doubtful a handful of bullets winging skyward would set off an avalanche, unless accompanied by whumping helicopter blades or the tremors of exploding dynamite. For the most part, snow slides on its own, prompted by natural elements like ice and sunshine and steep grades, way out there in backcountry.

Unfortunately that's where many skiers are going these days. Equipment is greatly improved; snowboards are now common. Skiers are whizzing past posted warning signs, dropping from helicopters in unmarked territory, crisscrossing slopes with first tracks where the margin for error is so slim, even the professionals are making mistakes. Where *fatal* avalanches are concerned, the causes break down like this:

Snowpack (1), Weather (2), Terrain (4), and Human (34), according to a study by the International Snow Science Workshop, which evaluated forty-one fatal avalanches for the decade between 1990 and 2000. Which brings us to this fairly obvious conclusion: Human beings are to blame for a huge proportion of avalanche deaths. A snowmobile travels where it shouldn't. A snowboarder feels like showing off. A skier is infected by adrenaline and that magnificent powder arcing behind like a controlled wave, sighing as the sugary froth touches down on her hat, shoulders, and back.

And soon the tumble of ice and snow is set off, bouncing over rock and cliff, flattening hundred-year-old evergreens and everything else in its path.

Mid-March. A spring snowstorm moved into the Hasliberg on a Sunday night, depositing at least a foot of brand-new powder in the valley and mountain surround. Monday, the snow was still fresh, so K.C.; his wife, Kathleen; and teenaged son, Rowan, headed up the lift for an afternoon ski. K.C. and Kathleen were teachers now and also served on the school's directorial team, the *Leitung*. Their son was visiting from college.

Tuesday, after Konferenz, the directors declared a ski day. The air was razor sharp, the sky brilliant, and within minutes word went out that classes were canceled. A scuffle and hoot rose in the large dining hall where everyone ate breakfast. K.C. had been asked to lead a small group of advanced student skiers off-piste. Nothing unusual about that. As they rode up together in the *Gondelbahn*, swinging some seventy feet above the ground, he sketched out their route. Monday had been sunny too. Snow on the south-facing slopes had no doubt melted, frozen overnight, creating a troublesome crust. And because it was late in the season, even west-facing inclines might have been affected. Thus the best place to find powder would be facing north.

Skiing in the Alps differs significantly from virtually anywhere in North America. Lifts take you far above the tree line to vast, unmarked areas, what would be considered backcountry in the United States except that there is so much more of it. After nearly four decades, K.C. was well accustomed to these wide-open stretches of white, their dips, rises, and angles. He'd led a group of students here just weeks earlier when the powder was fresh. The kids couldn't have been happier, gliding over the super smooth, heaven-beckoning surface.

On this particular day, they caught the T-bar to Winterhalde and a mountain the Ecole nicknamed Aurobindo Peak after Edith Geheeb's Indian friend who was once hopelessly lost hiking there. They aimed for untracked snow and at first stuck to the closer, more gradual slopes, laying down line over line, like strokes of longhand. After that was covered, K.C. decided to move farther along to Aurobindo and more untouched powder. They unhitched their skis and hiked to a ridge, higher and steeper, for the buttery descent. K.C. usually waited the requisite four or five days after a snowfall, which is how long it takes for the various layers to bond. Or he held off till someone else had tested the area and found it sturdy. But he never, ever, took students with him. That morning, for some reason, he set out after just two days. Not long enough.

Werner Munter is *the* avalanche expert—a bearded, wild-looking mountain guide out of Lohnstorf. His reputation skyrocketed after the period 1981 to 1991, when there were fifty-two avalanche deaths in less than ten professionally guided ski tours. Then Munter was motivated to invent a more reliable method of calculating risk factors in off-trail skiing, known as the three-by-three, or the Reduction Method. He aimed to reduce fatalities by half.

In Munter's system, three things come into play: conditions (snow pack and weather), terrain (angle, aspect, position), and human (group size and experience). As the facts change, these three factors are obsessively sifted and re-examined at three distinct levels: during the planning stage in the region, in the local area, and on the actual slope, thus the term three-by-three. Mathematicians, lawyers, scientists, engineers, and philosophers use a similar system when testing new theories. Highly dangerous conditions include the following: slopes on the northwest-north-northeast aspect; angle of thirty-five to forty-five degrees; few anchors (trees, large boulders); cliff, gully, funnel; and warming trend.

Because K.C. and Kathleen were family heads, they were required to eat breakfast, lunch, and dinner with students in dining hall. No need for both of them to be there at the same time, so they split the responsibility. A meal at home was welcome respite. He usually took the morning shift, but lately they'd switched off so she was the one present during daily announcements. Except that in this instance, she'd been called to the phone while the athletic director announced a ski day. Waiting for the clamor to subside, he warned that avalanche danger was extremely high on the steeper slopes. *Avoid those slopes*, he repeated, a message Kathleen would most certainly have conveyed to her husband, had she heard it. Like a scene out of Shakespeare, it was almost fated—the message never landed where it absolutely had to. Riding the Gondelbahn with eight keyed up students, K.C. simply wasn't thinking *avalanche*.

Imagine you are skiing at a managed resort. It's a theme park of perfectly packed trails winding in and out of the forest over moguls and minor jumps. There's a lookout restaurant at the top that serves hot chocolate and coffee. There are Poma, T-bar, and chair lifts leading in every possible direction. There's a hut that shelters the ski patrol who are all suited in bright orange parkas. You'll live forever. And this is the thought that warms you all over, that fills your brain as you feel the pull of something more challenging. Action gives way to more action, its own kind of somersaulting momentum. Perhaps there's nothing holding you back. Or maybe there's a rope strung between multiple warning signs clear as day—PROCEED AT YOUR OWN RISK, DANGER, RECOVERY FEE! You've seen the words so often they fail to sink in. Whether real or metaphorical, the far side of this meager barrier is off-piste, ungroomed, and possibly brutal, requiring you to think like a scientist if you want that long and healthy life. But what are the chances of that?

More likely, you'll take the risk via several mental shortcuts that nearly every human being falls prey to: Your friends are already heading that way and calling to you, *Come on! What are you waiting for?* If *they* feel safe, why shouldn't you? Or, you know that X is an expert skier and if *he* feels safe, why worry? You don't want to look like a coward; you may not have this incredible opportunity again. Or you were here a few days ago skiing this precise slope and nothing terrible happened. And, *you* are the expert and want to give your troops a good time, an adventure they'd never experience on the trails, powder falling like stardust and the incredible speed down.

The group reached the top of the ridge, seriously winded from the climb. They threw down their gear and took a short break, basking in the sun and the morning's utter pleasure. Ahead was the best run ever, steep and broad. One by one they stepped into board and ski bindings, grabbed their poles, itching to fly. There was little talk of conditions or the safest route down or even who should go first. Once they were ready to ski, no one wanted to hang out and chat. K.C. shouted, "Okay, have fun!" And took off.

When wind approaches a snow-covered ridge, it forms drifts on the lee side called cornices, extending beyond the rock into thin air, forming icy sculptures as graceful as fishtails. Skiers instinctively wander to an edge to begin their descent or take in the scenery, but the safest spot is actually far enough back so the view is obscured. Cornices break off earlier than one would assume, taking the skier down and setting an avalanche in motion. Two students were standing on the ridge within three feet of each other, waiting to take their run. There was a loud snap, like a giant cracker split between the two, and one—we'll call her Noriko—dropped fast, disappearing with an almost soundless whoop right in the middle of her sentence. She was gone.

Ahead of the students, K.C. took two or three turns and then bunny-hopped down the steepest section of the slope. Suddenly everything was moving. He immediately thought, *What the . . . ?* Then, *I'm going to die.* The powdery surface unhitched from the hard pack beneath, broke into huge rectangular sections sliding faster and faster. No time to consider the kids behind him; besides, he had no idea where they were. He tried skiing over to the right, but within seconds his bindings popped open. Soon he was sitting upright, shooting down the mountain, head above the snow parting and plunging around him. It was a nightmare version of that controlled wave: descending a flight of stairs on a surfboard followed by a ton of frozen water. But he could see the sky, lots of it, and thought, *Maybe I can ride this out*—the slope eventually flattened out and rose up again on the other side, right? To survive he would simply stand up.

Then he hit a freefall. Alarmed, he rapidly retraced the area's geography. *Where's the cliff?* Turns out, there's a smaller ridge that juts in from a short distance away. He'd shot over that like a cannonball. His arms flew up. He landed with a jolt, hard on his heels. Momentum carried him forward and now he lay face down, flat out, the snow quickly following with a *fwump*. He was buried.

I heard later Hannah headed down on her snowboard maybe six feet or so behind me. She was caught in the avalanche too. But her bindings didn't open, so she stayed on her board and passed me over this jump. She landed, and I landed pretty much right on top of her. I heard screaming but assumed it came from the girls at the top of the hill. I felt something touch my leg, but figured it was an animal. She was right underneath me.

From the moment of fracture, an avalanche moves fast: from zero to forty or even eighty miles per hour in roughly fifteen seconds. Not the time to assume a zazen attitude. Those with presence of mind will tuck their heads into their elbows, or cross their arms over their face, creating an air pocket. The larger the pocket, the better chance of breathing. But who has presence of mind in split-second intervals? Anyway, K.C. thought he was going to make it until the freefall. By chance, his helmet held back the oncoming flow and created a crucial opening around his face, while boulders of snow solidified around him, rock solid as the avalanche stopped. He was encased in cement and began to panic, breathing hard and fast, adrenaline working its high-octane fuel on his heart. *Now* was the time for meditation. Within four minutes, he could lose consciousness. Twenty-five minutes later, half of avalanche victims are dead. At 130 minutes, the number jumps to 97 percent.

Moving even an inch was out of the question, except for his right hand, which convinced him he might be near the surface. Perhaps he could wiggle that hand to create an air pocket, even a tunnel. That hand was now working the snow. For the moment he had enough air. He calmed down, realizing he wouldn't suffocate. He took the time to mentally examine his body from head to toe and realized he was pretty comfortable: no broken bones from the tumble, no lacerations, no hugely awkward position like a leg bent into a boomerang behind him. Bleeding didn't appear to be a danger. Also, dozens of skiers saw the avalanche; it occurred within sight of the chairlift and several slopes nearby. Perhaps his hand was even visible from the surface. He felt confident and light, as if a team of rescuers was already lifting him up.

The minutes passed quickly. He might have been buried a quarter-hour, even half, without any sign of rescue. Cold seeped through his clothes, skin, muscle and fat, numbing his extremities. Those little muscle contractions that usually kept him warm were not in play. His body temperature was dropping and that triggered more panic: *I'm going to freeze to death before anyone arrives.* Then a stubborn streak kicked in: No, he was *not* finished. Not with his wife, the kids. Not with the school. A thousand similar thoughts. He tried shouting, but the sound was muffled. How could anyone hear him? He spent a few more seconds struggling to break out, grunting and twisting till he realized making a dent was not only impossible; it was stupid. Better not to waste his energy. Just before he passed out and began to dream, he heard a helicopter. *Thank God*, he thought, *they're covering the mountain with infrared scanners. They'll find my body and pick me up soon.*

He woke up at the hospital in Bern.

At the Ecole, students are allowed to ski freely in established areas, but there are also *Angebote*, "other options," such as Aurobindo Peak, for level five and six skiers and snowboarders. Hearing that her husband intended to take a group off trail, and who among the students was planning to go along, Kathleen decided she was better suited for a less advanced group, headed by Phillip, another director. Their group took the Hohbühl lift up and skied down. Conditions were strange and she didn't enjoy it much; nevertheless, she headed toward the lift again and passed through the turnstile for another run. At that moment, Phillip's cell phone buzzed. She watched him closely as he took in the news of the accident, both of them trembling. They cut through the line and rode up toward the peak, where she immediately located the avalanche to the right: *There it is.* She slipped off the lift, skied closer to the scene, and burst into tears. Even from a distance, Kathleen was certain her husband was buried. He'd been wearing a red jacket and orange helmet and that particular combination was the only one missing on the slope.

You would think the order of rescue would place an avalanche victim at the top of the to-do list, but actually it's the reverse: rescuer, other survivors, then the buried person or persons—an ideal opportunity to put aside one's compassion for the human species and think "me first." The victim may be fine, or may have already suffocated, but rescuers must be safe or they are no good to anyone. There's snow above the avalanche that has yet to fall, known as hangfire. There are also adjacent slopes poised in identical conditions, ripe for a slide. In a sport relished for its speed—scenery whizzing by, wind and sun flying against the face—going slow is imperative for rescue. No one wants a new set of victims, or a mass of helpful souls trampling about, with vast areas over- or underexplored. Were there witnesses? Any partially buried skiers? That would offer a clue.

Before she fell, Noriko had been standing off to the right, a slight distance from the main slide. At its initial fracture, the avalanche slipped below to the left and little snow accumulated behind her. She came to a stop on the level, just short of the cliff, arm raised, a pink glove clearly visible. She could also see sky, a sizable blue swatch above her, so she knew she wasn't going to suffocate. One of her friends zipped down to the station to get help. Two others skied over to the glove but, scared to death of another slide, they stood frozen to the spot, not sure of what to do next. The girl was buried up to her forehead and they couldn't just yank her out by her arm and escape to safety. In a fairly calm frame of mind Noriko took charge, advising them to take off their snowboards and use them as shovels to dig.

It's helpful to know that even the pros can make a mess of a search. There's adrenaline, altruism, the urge to be a hero, not to mention the clock, ticking off those seconds. REGA (Search and Rescue) arrived on the scene pretty quickly, transporting eleven dog teams, each consisting of handler and animal. Two helicopters flew back and forth constantly refreshing with new teams. A ski patrol organized search groups, and other skiers came by to help. Several dozen volunteers probed the surface—ten in a row—all proceeding slowly, one step at a time, often penetrating the snow six meters down. At first they focused their search in the area before the drop-off because that's where Noriko was found. No one realized K.C. and Hannah had pitched over the cliff and because of this they lost a lot of time. In hindsight, it might have been smarter to hold everybody back, let the dogs do their job first—too many distracting scents and the trail was no doubt very faint. Finally, a dog located someone.

Instinct tells us to begin shoveling from the top down, but that would compress the snow, making it harder to lift and even more difficult for the victim to breathe. Also, the shortest path might be horizontal. These rescuers knew what they were doing and began to dig slightly downhill of the site, a tunnel shaped like a V. Every five minutes or so, someone would relieve the point digger in the same way bike racers take turns in the lead.

Kathleen avoided the hubbub and skied off to one side, crouched down, and distilled her attention down to just one thing—trying to make some kind of connection to her husband. She purposefully did not look at her watch. She'd lived in the area long enough to know every second counts in an avalanche. The likelihood he'd survive was slipping fast. A couple of students skied over to support her. "We're going find him," they promised. Others were simply hysterical. She just wanted to be alone, away from anyone's panic or false confidence.

She remembers whispering—"If you want to go, K.C., it's up to you. No question, I have my druthers. I would rather you stuck around. But I'm not going to hold you."

Then: "Well, maybe that was a bit too generous."

The excavating took forever. Forever. She remained unwilling to watch the worst news unreel in stop-action motion. A minister from Hohfluh walked over to her and softly inquired: "Do you want to say goodbye here, or closer to your husband?"

She snapped at him: "You don't even know he's dead yet."

Finally, three things happened: a student ran over to say she'd seen K.C. but couldn't determine if he was alive or dead, just blue. Another reported he'd moved—one arm, maybe a leg. Now Kathleen skied hurriedly to the site and watched as rescuers pulled her husband out and loaded him onto the sled. His head shifted side to side and he was moaning loud and clear, unconscious, but alive. That was the most mellifluous sound she'd heard in a lifetime.

A helicopter carried him off, along with two pilots and four doctors, heading toward Bern. Rescuers were still digging around and below where K.C. lay. They soon found Hannah, buried underneath the site. She'd landed on her back, face up, toes pointing toward the ridge above. Did she have time to extend her arms, clear an air pouch around her face, or was she already wearing that deadly ice mask? Her mouth must have rapidly filled with snow and surely she'd suffocated, but no one gave up and paramedics worked for what seemed like a long time. The director of search operations announced she'd be flown to a hospital with special equipment in Lucerne, though he admitted the girl had less than a 20 percent chance of surviving. He and every adult present knew it was over, but he thought it important to give the students a sliver of hope. No one wanted dozens of distraught teenagers on their hands. A friend drove Kathleen and two sons to Bern, where her husband lay in intensive care. A very, very sweet reunion.

K.C. woke up in the hospital with numerous staff bustling around him. He'd never been so cold in his life. So very cold, he was feeling kind of pissed off. Why hadn't they covered him with a blanket? "Would someone please get a blanket?" Of course physicians and nurses alike had used all sort of high-tech equipment to raise his body temperature, which was roughly eighty-seven degrees when he arrived, ten degrees below normal. He'd passed through a warming chamber in the emergency room, then on to intensive care, where one nurse, a chatty fellow, was assigned to him exclusively. He brought orange and apple juice, and after a while K.C. felt fine. It had been a huge adventure, but all's well that ends well, and he figured they'd be releasing him shortly. The nurse pressed his shoulder into the bed ever so gently and said, "Nope. We're going to keep you overnight. Keep an eye on you." His heartbeat was a little shaky and they wanted to monitor him on the ECG, a precaution that would continue after he left the place.

The family visited that evening, but before they even walked into his room, Kathleen pulled her two sons aside to make sure they agreed: "This isn't really our family style, but I'm not inclined to tell him the truth about Hannah just yet." Then they hurried over to K.C.'s bedside and closed around him, all of them in tears. The next day, with more time to visit, Kathleen asked her husband if he'd known Hannah was also caught in the avalanche. He had not. For now, that was as far as she dared go, even when he asked outright, "She's dead, isn't she?" Indeed, school directors had confirmed the death from the hospital in Lucerne. The girl's temperature had been seventy-seven degrees upon arrival, far lower than K.C.'s.

From the outside at least, Kathleen could hardly believe how unfazed her husband appeared, given the magnitude of the experience. He seemed wrapped in layers of cotton, most likely muted by shock. When enough time had passed, the family drove to Lucerne and walked down a silvery hospital corridor into the morgue. The technician opened a small steel door and pulled Hannah's body out. Just like in the movies she was covered with a white drape, drawn back to reveal her face. K.C.'s first thought was that the technician had made a mistake. Hannah was an outdoorsy person, healthy and beaming. Here she appeared waxen, oddly posed. He asked to be alone. That's when he let go, sobbing and broken for what seemed like hours. As crazy as it sounds, he'd been hoping the accident could somehow be reversed. But not now.

▲▲▲

Hanging on the walls of the Twing ski shop are gorgeously produced posters of serene mountain slopes blanketed in snow. Undulating tracks emboss the expanse, carved by tiny red-helmeted skiers.

Who wouldn't want to ski there? Who wouldn't want to live there? One catches my eye—yet another stretch of white set against a shocking blue sky. But there's a difference. From a distance it might be texture: perhaps creases in the paper. Closer up, the topography breaks into a dozen jagged gouges, as if swiped by giant bear claws. There's some kind of insect in the left-hand corner. No, it's not a bug; it's a lone skier, the one who set the snow in motion on his second or third turn. Unfettered man, skis tucked into a widening crevice of broken ice, hoping against hope to avoid the thunder to his right, which, as he cannot see, loops left, directly under his path down the hill. The photograph is at least fifteen years old. Was there a rescue team? What slip of thinking led the skier here? Is there a future beyond this scene?

Aftermath

Finally the story returns to the panorama from which it started, but though everything looks the same, the eye that sees them is full of memories and no longer disinterested. The mountain is not only beautiful but dangerous and lovable because its dangers have been met with courage. The road over the col is no longer taken for granted, but is seen as a triumph of the human will to neighborliness over an indifferent or hostile nature which would keep men estranged.
—ADALBERT STIFTER, *Rock Crystal*

Der Blick: March 14, 2006

Black day in the white Alps: Avalanches in canton Bern, Freiburg, and Graubünden, where several skiers were buried. Tragically, one died, a fifteen year old from Aargau.

It had been snowing in the last few days as if there were no tomorrow—with gale-force winds—the perfect recipe for highly dangerous avalanche conditions in the Alps. In spite of warnings there were some who just could not stay away. This happened today. A group of seven or eight skiers steered into the area around Käserstatt/Winterhalde in the Berner Oberlander community of Hasliberg at approximately ten in the morning. Three of them, one man and two women, were buried as they were snowboarding. One woman was immediately rescued. And after three hours of intense rescue efforts the other two were found, but they were seriously injured. The search and rescue effort was launched immediately and included over a hundred professional and civil personnel, two helicopters, and eleven avalanche dog teams, digging in up to six meters of avalanche cover. A care team tended to the needs of the less injured but for one fifteen year old nothing was to be done. She died at the hospital upon arrival.

Philipp Hostettler in his sixties looks very much the mountain man. He's lost the blond highlights of his teenage years at the Ecole, but it's obvious he's still in great shape and his English is decent. He's one of the dedicated half-dozen who returned after graduation to teach, to set up an apprenticeship program, to act as professional advisor for special education students, and to serve as director of the sports division. With mountains all around, he sits under an umbrella on the Hotel Gletscherblick's patio. His wife, Marie-Anne, sits opposite, chiming in anytime Philipp pauses to sip his beer.

Der Blick, he says, is "street paper," a penny dreadful similar to our *National Enquirer*. "By the rescue system, the press is notified, and this newspaper was the first arriving. We couldn't even give them our comment. They got the scoop and blew the whole thing up. Because Switzerland is the place where everything that happens, happens in the mountains, an accident is very soon published, in the TV and so on. When it happens with the kids, it's even more like that. The other newspapers were different. We could organize more, what was said. And we had to protect the students and the staff, because the press arrived at the school looking for information."

He said Hannah was a charismatic young woman with an infectious laugh and optimism that drew other students and teachers close. She'd suffered the death of her father at an early age and everyone agreed this made her capable of great empathy. After Hannah's death, her family and many best friends became first priority to the school. Then the directors turned to caring for the rest of the school and met very briefly to figure out just how to get through the next day. Two clergy from a nearby town immediately offered their services. Psychologists arrived from the big cities. And there were rituals already in place, including a special Andacht—with readings, music, and communal sharing of grief, fear, and anger.

Die Leitung had two things in their favor. A long vacation was coming up with more time to heal and plan. Philipp, a ski tour guide in addition to all his other duties, got back to the basics, recalling as much detail as he could from the accident, including where and when they might have gone wrong. Then he called a good lawyer from Brienz. It wasn't long before Frederic, director of outdoor safety, and Philipp were among the accused.

Hannah's mother, Birgit, could easily have filed a lawsuit. Instead, she had an unusually enlightened reaction to the accident. She is an artist, a compassionate woman, and yes, she endured an excruciating grief. But she was also convinced from the very beginning that Hannah's soul chose its own path. Not the path Birgit desired for her daughter, but something she could eventually come to accept. Birgit never blamed anyone, not even K.C., and her support was one reason why the school was able to push past the devastating event. Her eldest, Stefan, was the first to attend the Ecole, and later her youngest, Nicole, wanted to apply too, despite the avalanche, despite the loss of her big sister. Eventually Birgit agreed to this and the girl went on to graduate successfully.

▲▲▲

Herr Lüthi ducks slightly as he opens the door to his small apartment behind Haupthaus. His limbs move slowly in his eighty-sixth year. Natalie passed away months ago and there's a marked melancholy in his manner. Yet despite the thousands of students revolving in and out of his long life at the school, he greets me warmly, as if remembering me well: "Sahrah. How güt to see you again."

Armin has a favorite chair by the window overlooking the Wetterhorn. He needs a glass of water, a cup of tea, which I fetch from the small kitchen. He unfolds the blanket on his lap and pulls his chair slightly closer to the table. His voice still soothes, warm and measured, for here in this well-worn body the provocative theories of Paul Geheeb and the practicality of cofounder Edith are peaceably settled. The Lüthis made sure those theories worked in practice for more than fifty years.

Armin dips and swirls his tea bag one last time, wraps it around his spoon, then squeezes. A few drops land on the table and he puckers his lips with vexation. He pulls a shredded tissue from his sleeve and dabs. I can't help but feel sad and a little ashamed at my eagerness to get it all down before he dies. His sentences don't connect and dwindle into somewhere. I don't dare bring up the accident, but our conversation— so scattershot—eventually zeros in on just that.

"You know," he begins. "I mean, sometimes I now think why did I stay here at the Ecole for so long? We had this avalanche disaster a few years ago. And K.C. was the leader of this group where the accident happened. He should NOT have done it. It was quite clear. Well, he was sentenced to, not to prison but to, I don't know, five years of. . . . If he had made another mistake he would have gone to prison. I mean it was . . . he is a funny . . . he is a wonderful guy. But it is strange . . . perhaps he had no feeling for the danger. And since then, I mean, okay, it was of course in the school's interest to talk about security and safety and things like this, but we were also pressured from the cities. Now security is so important. Our hikes are planned from the first moment to the last moment. And we must know where they spend the night, and we must have done this hike before. It's different."

Armin can only shake his head. Nearly seven decades had passed since the school's only other mortality at Versoix.

▲▲▲

K.C. came home from the hospital on a Thursday, two days after the avalanche. And directly after that an officer from Meiringen arrived at the school to interview him. Whenever a death of any kind occurs, the local police are immediately involved. Kathleen wanted more recovery time for her husband because she felt he was not quite himself, but rather "in the clouds." It wasn't just K.C. she was protecting. She'd been living one of the most difficult ordeals of her life, forced into making executive decisions without her best friend. But the officer explained that in his experience, people often felt relief after talking. And of course it's better if the story's fresh. K.C. was willing. Kathleen could see he thought everything was "just fine," when nothing at all was "just fine."

Later, the couple went down to the Meiringen station for further questioning. The police were very professional, not the least bit accusatory. They allowed Kathleen to be present. Somebody took notes, typed them up, and read them back to make sure they were accurate, section by section. Kathleen's chief concern was K.C.'s openness and self-deprecation—afraid he would take too much on his cap. She remembered explicitly reminding him: "Now listen, you only have to answer their questions." She didn't want him to lie of course; they'd get through if he focused on telling the truth as he experienced it. She just didn't want him to reveal his inner processing. But the questioning went smoothly and was manageable for both. After two and a half years, the case finally came to trial. The charge was involuntary manslaughter, though the German term translates a tad more harshly—*Fahrlässiger Tötung* or "negligent killing."

If you live in the Hasliberg and commit a crime, you'll face judgment in the Interlaken *Kloster und Schloss*, a converted castle and monastery just steps away from the river Aare. First mention of the abbey dates to 1133. At one point, 30 Augustinian priests, 20 lay brothers, and 350 nuns lived here. The buildings have been used as a hospital for the poor, a granary, and storage for wine. Now the monastic area serves as an administrative center for the district, or *Zivilstandsamt Oberland Ost*, where numerous documents are obtained, including birth and death certificates, paternity claims, adoption certificates, same-sex partner registration, and name changes. Tucked away on the ground floor, there's a room with a low tray ceiling accented in grays. A huge Dutch stove fills one corner, but it's too pretty and ancient to be in use and, indeed, I spot radiators under the windows. The lighting is soft. Even empty, the space feels cozy, though an enormous desk opposes four chairs for the accused, each upholstered in black. Additional seating for family and friends fills the rest of the room. The desk is bare, save three objects: a leather portfolio embossed with the words *Zivilstandskreis Oberland Ost*, a heart-shaped velour box, and something that looks like a bride's withered bouquet in a vase. Later I learn the room is now used for weddings.

Here a judge faced three Ecole directors who remained calm and centered throughout, refusing to point a finger at anyone else. They answered questions truthfully and carefully, mindful of each other, friends whose friendship had been seriously challenged by the accident. It was exemplary behavior, the result of years teaching in a school that emphasizes honesty, self-reliance, and sensitivity to others. All three men narrated, separately and with impeccable detail, their versions of the events leading to Hannah's death. Their stories fit together nicely, as closely knit as anything could be. Precision, rightness, completeness. The Swiss ideal applies to more than train schedules and cleanliness. It pertains to the moral life as well.

Several avalanche experts were brought in, including Werner Munter, who had trained Philipp in ski touring. Though officially retired, Munter often stepped in to advise during complicated trials. All the consultants reviewed the Ecole's safety procedures and deemed them solid, but Munter's opinion mattered the most. It was a turning point.

The judge was a relatively young man but sharp and fair. He also had a flair for drama, exclaiming that Philipp and Frederic should never have been accused in the first place, a powerful statement that ultimately led to their acquittal. A more worrisome question, and perhaps the weakest point in the case, hovered around K.C.'s internal training and whether it *was* adequate. True, he hadn't completed an off-campus, certifying course in avalanches. But the judge deftly skipped over that issue and moved on to the others, arguing very clearly, very patiently, why Philipp and Frederic were innocent. If K.C. had been motivated, he could have objected, spread the guilt around a bit, but he wasn't in the least bit interested. It was bad enough watching his friends go through two and a half years of uncertainty. When the judge finally cleared the two men on the final charge, all three stood next to each other and clasped hands.

Where K.C. was concerned, the judge asked the right questions and could see that this man had never waivered from the truth, beginning with his very first interview with the police. K.C. was clearly a man of character, and the judge asked several times, dumbfounded: "What's your salary again?" Nope, not in it for the money. He'd dedicated his life to educating children, meant no harm, and yet, this tragedy occurred, which caused him great suffering. K.C. was sentenced to the absolute minimum allowable by law: two years of probation, during which time, if any other crimes were committed, the consequences would be far more serious. He was not obliged to pay any fines, and legal costs were covered by the school's insurance policies. Later, K.C.'s lawyer took him aside to say, "You know, we could probably appeal and go for innocent." But K.C. refused: "That wouldn't be right. I'm not completely innocent, and I'm willing to take the consequences." There was no way around it: he'd been thrown off track by the excitement of the moment and neglected to consider the hazards, which unquestionably resulted in Hannah's death.

Wrong and right, dark and light. Contrast is important to both moral and visual systems. One person steals; another wouldn't dare. Where there are stars, the night appears a deeper black. Without them we have *Eigengrau* (intrinsic gray), our vision in the absence of light. This is where the unclassifiable falls. In his assessments of avalanche danger, Werner Munter noted a 10 percent area of doubt—things you have no control over, cannot see, and cannot predict. That's why risk is always present in off-trail skiing.

For me that 10 percent lay somewhere wedged between the following series of events: The avalanche warning *was* issued at breakfast. K.C. and Kathleen were *not* there to hear it. K.C. *was* asked, as per usual, if he could take a group off-trail, and he agreed, taking with him a group of students who were also expert skiers. Frederic and Philipp *knew* he was not equipped with certified avalanche training. Finally, K.C. *did* lead his kids to a dangerous slope, reflecting on little other than sunshine and good powder. Perhaps all parties were under the spell of an impossible impatience. Whether due to a lack of snow and deficit of ski days, long weeks cooped up in classrooms—when the powder finally arrived, it made everyone unusually keyed up. In the chaos of finishing breakfast, clearing tables, gathering into groups, and the thwacking forest of skis and poles, K.C.'s only consideration was reaching that lovely white stuff as quickly as possible.

▲▲▲

Shortly after the accident Kathleen attended Mitarbeiter Konferenz to request the use of a car. The atmosphere was tense and she soon realized that she could in no way allow her husband to return to the Ecole, not yet. They both needed distance from the school, a safe place where they could ease back into things. Natalie suggested time off in a Ferienwohnung a few miles down the Reutistrasse, which proved to be the right medicine. The apartment overlooked the mountains and the couple was able to control their social encounters and ensure they were mostly positive. Their sons visited often, and so did members of their Ecole family. But faculty, many of them close friends, stayed away. Later they discovered directors had made it clear that the couple were recuperating under a psychologist's care, and best *not* to visit. In fact, they were under no care whatsoever.

"I was feeling worthless, irredeemable," K.C. recalled. "I wanted to make it up somehow—impossible, I know. My first impulse was: get right back to work, teach my classes, and give all I possibly could to these young people. But they wouldn't let me. I was really shocked by that. It was almost the end of term. There were two or three days of classes left and I wanted to finish up the chemistry I'd been teaching most of the year. One colleague said, 'If he teaches, I'm quitting.'"

The accident was traumatic enough. Its aftermath erupted and unfurled at the Ecole, a kind of sequel to the avalanche, blindsiding the couple. They returned from Reuti and again took up residence in Waldhaus with their family but the only place Kathleen felt secure was in her living room. Anytime she stepped outside, she tripped through a minefield.

There had been unsettled gripes even before the accident. Two faculty were not subtle in their ambition. They'd reached a point in their careers where they too should be bosses on the Leitung and wanted more authority. Disagreements and confrontations were commonplace. Another teacher recalled an incident that foreshadowed K.C.'s "carelessness." Driving a group of students to a basketball game in Lucerne he nearly collided with a guardrail—a dangerous driver too! Whether this particular event happened or not, the avalanche turned catalyst, churning all sorts of tensions to the surface. A faction of vocal and motivated teachers felt it imperative he quit the directorship. They were genuinely worried the school would not recover from the disaster. And no colleague involved with the death of a student should remain in that position. He'd committed the unforgivable and must be fired. Which is not technically the law in Switzerland, as one board member noted, though eventually they did relieve him of all directorial duties. There also was the question of whether he should be allowed to teach again. Ever. This shunning added yet another layer of shame and grief.

▲▲▲

Overall, the Ecole's response to the tragedy was quick and thorough. Parents were continually updated with nuances and the kind of detail no penny dreadful bothered to touch. If they'd lost confidence or faith in the school, they were welcome to pull their children without financial consequence. Only one family did, a Taiwanese father who was seriously spooked by the incident. A psychological consultant from Zurich was highly impressed, noting that the Ecole's actions served as a kind of model in crisis management. Some faculty weren't so sure: "Oh, no question. The students were showered with support. One counselor from England who used to teach here flew in to work with the English speakers. We had priests. We had therapists. Family heads checked in with their young people every single day—Someone looks a little shaky. What's his temperature right now? We had special rituals and gatherings. The kids had a zillion people assisting in the healing process. But there was nothing particular for the adults. Anyone who wanted to could request a therapist, but no general admission: OK guys, we've had a real shock. Who's going to help us? We did an amazing job of taking care of the kids and a horrible job of taking care of ourselves. I mean, think about it—after the mass slaying at Virginia Tech, faculty were required to attend counseling three times a week. This was the one real flaw in the Ecole response."

Kathleen was more interested in pedagogy than firefighting, as she puts it, though she'd been groomed for the directorship from the very beginning. She preferred focusing on preventative programs, such as peer counseling or drug and alcohol intervention. To that end, she'd retired from the Leitung the year before the accident. The other directors rearranged tasks and responsibilities so that they could squeeze down from five to four members, but now this—K.C.'s departure resulted in a serious gap. Kathleen volunteered to step back in. Who else would they ask? She knew the job inside and out. She would represent K.C. and seemed like the best candidate to help the school carry on in a rocky situation.

But any recovery issue affecting K.C. also affected Kathleen. She was far too preoccupied with healing and suddenly had to deal with admissions and hiring and college applications. Her heart wasn't in it. And many teachers were still fuming. She served for another three years, suffered a breakdown, then took an eighteen-month sick leave.

▲▲▲

K.C.: "Letters, cards, phone calls, whatever, poured in. Especially from students. They were full of love, how much I meant to them, stuff like that. At first they were painful to read and I put them aside. But the letters kept coming, and after a while I started to feel, okay, 'I guess I can't be all bad.' And a couple of Japanese students organized all their friends to make a thousand cranes, a waterfall of colorful origami that hung in our apartment for a long time. Now the accident trickles in and out of my life. It's part of me. I can go weeks without thinking about it—well, no, I can't. I can go for days without thinking about it. I can go for weeks without any heavy emotional impact. Then a phase will come where it'll hit me again, and then I feel either fearful or sad. Mostly sad."

Some things you cannot forget: furrows in your memory, packed, and preserved with snow.

K.C. and Kathleen remained in Goldern until 2011, when they made their final move to Meiringen. Kathleen began a family coaching business. After eighteen years at the school, which he now describes as "intense and exhausting," K.C. wasn't sure where to go next. Teaching at a Swiss public school wasn't an option since he didn't have the credentials. So he felt fortunate when a job opened up at a local home for the mentally disabled—a comparatively restful but valuable vocation. Later, he went for certification.

Those ambitious faculty? They became bosses elsewhere and new faculty have replaced them.

▲▲▲

Me, Kathleen, and a dog named Phoebe catch the gondola from Meiringen to Reuti, then switch to a smaller capsule for the ride up to Bidmi, where a half-toasted conductor flirts rather flagrantly. We disembark and set out on a gravel path. Once past the restaurant, Kathleen unsnaps Phoebe's leash to let her roam. The trail is not difficult, looping back and forth till we turn right toward Aurobindo Peak. Cow paths, famous for leading summer hikers off course, form a pattern of horizontal stripes across the humped mountain. We circle round to the north face, rough with granite, thorny bush, and something called *Alpenerle*, or green alder, advancing down the slope like a scrappy battalion. They are the bane of farmers, these colonists of scree and stony hillsides, one of only a few species that can survive rockslides and avalanches. Kathleen can testify to their resilience as she and her Ecole family once had great difficulty bushwhacking through them.

Here we scramble, sometimes on all fours, careful of our footwork toward the outcropping where K.C. and Hannah were carried, far to the right of where they intended to ski. The terrain for them was uniform, cold, and white. Nothing like the irregular ground we're covering now. My lungs don't fill as easily at this altitude, but Kathleen is well used to it. Meanwhile Phoebe has raced down toward a muddy pond, where she's found a duck to chase through the water. Up and over two ridges, a marmot lets out a whistle to warn of our approach and soon we're standing on the very spot the two skiers were buried by the avalanche. But I can't visualize a winter scene, even with squinting, the area is so broken up, so full of depths and pockets and stumpy evergreens. We descend, then partly climb an adjacent hill, where I have a much better view.

Not the long slide I imagined. Not even half the distance. Couldn't have lasted more than a few seconds. Kathleen tells me it's a myth that slides only happen in places where other slides have occurred. No sign of that here anyway. No mountain runway so steep nothing will grow. No thick groove flaring at the base like a dustpan. Just another fact they learned a little too late, along with Munter's three-by-three system and the importance of carrying a homing device, even a cell phone.

And the mud, stray leaves, blue gentian, buried grubs and worms and other burrowing insects—what do they retain of the accident, of the hours-long press of Hannah's body against the earth? Is there even a slight indentation, worthy of those white crosses you see on American highways embellished with small plastic bouquets? Not in Switzerland, where tossing biodegradable cremains off a hill is strictly verboten.

Slopes on the northwest-north-northeast aspect; angle of thirty-five to forty-five degrees; gullies or funnels (at least three); and very few anchors (mature trees, large boulders). All that is pretty clear now, even in the summer.

▲▲▲

In 1976, philosopher Bernard Williams came up with the expression "moral luck," which counters the idea, inspired by Kant, that morality is immune from luck. Say you are walking down a crowded street to the subway and a woman from behind slams into you, causing you to stumble onto the cement. All eyes will be on her for her selfish, clumsy move. Or was she to blame? Perhaps she too was pushed? How far back in the chain of events would we have to go before we can locate the perpetrator of an immoral act?

And what about circumstance? Had nature lined up a safer set of conditions, Hannah wouldn't have died, and life in the Ecole would have continued without trauma and heartache. But snow is neutral, indifferent, subject to constantly shifting weather conditions. The best we can do is to assess the risks in off-piste skiing and issue a warning. K.C. missed that warning. Surely K.C. did not *intend* to lead his group into danger. Should we refrain from moral judgment when much in this situation depended on chance?

Luck figures in our genetics too. K.C. was blessed with devout leadership skills, empathy, diligence, and perhaps a little daring. What element of his physical, emotional, and moral constitution was he acting on? Was it within his control? Maybe not.

The Ecole emphasizes two important human qualities: self-reliance and responsibility to the community. Their educational system works toward a balance of both. It's safe to say this balance is never perfect. A teenager is derailed by a brief crush or night of drunkenness. An adult is swept away by chirping young people locking in their bindings. The trigger can be good news, bad news, or no news at all. It can begin with great satisfaction or an overwhelming ennui and longing for an event, anything to distract and stir the heart. Anyone who works with adolescents knows their energy is contagious. In fact, teachers in high schools often choose their profession because they haven't quite abandoned their own adolescence. For a few perilous minutes K.C. soaked up the all-out pleasure and surging hormones of his students. Their excitement aroused in him a sliver of self from long ago, when he wasn't in charge. He was a teenager momentarily sailing along without the guardrails, safety straps, and regulations he'd acquired in maturation. It was a temporary slip of attention, his desire to make people happy overtaking his responsibility to protect. Haven't we all been there, at least once?

Suddenly common sense becomes something else, and good judgment heads for the hills. Anything can happen, especially following a snowstorm when most avalanches occur, under dazzling sunlight and unimpeachable blue skies.

The Twin Cities 〰 *Sehnsucht*

A naked man, carved in wood, is folded over himself into a kind of chest-down fetal position. Perhaps he is trapped in a cave or under the weight of a ton of quick-frozen water. Maybe he is sleeping, or just beginning his day.

At first glance he resembles a gentle rise, a hillock—the only object inside a gray, otherwise empty landscape. There are ribs like the stone creases formed by retreating glaciers. There is the spine, a knotty ridge down the middle of his back. There is the whisper of a hand, four fingers emerging from inside his body-clench. And one beautifully rounded ear.

Easy to imagine the forces at work: snow, mud, rain, punishing wind. But we don't see the weather, internal or external. The wood is well sanded, light in color. Lighter still is a thin coating of what looks like vernix, that protective, chalky matter easing an infant's passage from the birth canal. The hairless, nameless figure seems pressed between mortal extremes: not exactly newborn, not exactly dying. The master woodcarver is Bruno Walpoth. He named his sculpture *Nostalgia*.

July 10, 2006. The Ninth International Woodcarvers Symposium opens with much ado in the village of Brienz, just a short ride (ninety minutes by borrowed bike or eleven minutes by train) along the Haslital from Meiringen. The Grandhotel Giessbach rises majestically above the aqua-green waters and in the center of town sits a museum dedicated to woodcarving, an art that dates in this area back to the first century. The celebration has begun. Its subject is Sehnsucht. Federal Councilor Christoph Blocher steps up to the podium and delivers

Nostalgia, sculpture in lindenwood by Bruno Walpoth.

from his notes a speech remarkable enough to be reproduced on multiple websites. Here is an excerpt:

> Ladies and Gentlemen,
>
> It is my pleasure to welcome you, the participants in this exclusive symposium, here today and to extend to you the greetings of the Federal Council. This year's symposium in Brienz has not picked an easy theme: woodcarvers from all over the world have been asked to express their idea of Sehnsucht in a work of art. What is the meaning of Sehnsucht? Sehnsucht is one of those German words almost impossible to translate adequately. . . . Tender longing goes hand in hand with the painful knowledge that the thing longed for will never quite be attained. Indeed, you even get the feeling that the granting of an eagerly awaited wish could immediately bring about the destruction of the desired object. . . . The feeling of Sehnsucht is universal. And it is in the nonverbal means of expression—in painting, music, and the visual arts—that this universal nature can be seen to best advantage.

The word can be split into two parts: first *Sehne* (tendon), proof the concept comes from the fabric of our musculature—what keeps us upright, stretching, reaching. Then *Sucht*, for addiction or obsession. All together Sehnsucht: a longing for a point in time, but not necessarily a specific time. A vague location that may resemble Hawaii, Australia, Tibet, or somewhere that only exists in the imagination.

In the city of Heimweh, there's a clear sight line aiming directly toward home, fixing on a specific house and family. Sehnsucht's searchlight is restless, doesn't know where exactly to land, and sweeps the sky fruitlessly. It points skyward toward stars, planets, or beyond.

You want it, but you can't have it. You'll never have it as long as you live. The object of Sehnsucht may change over a lifetime. It's even possible to hunger after something you're standing right next to if once upon a time it allowed a release from self-consciousness, a floating outside your unwieldy, earthly body. You've never been the same since.

The Portuguese call it *saudade*, the Welsh *hiraeth*, Russians have *toska* (a favorite of Nabokov's), Romanians *dor*, and in Finnish it's *kaiho*. Yet for every human, the wanting is unique.

"Yes," says the politician. "You may find something here impressively constructed, even moving. But inevitably there will be disconnect, an inside voice wagering: that's really beautiful, but not what Sehnsucht is like for me. No earthbound work of art can satisfy the Sehnsucht of anyone other than the maker, and probably not even him or her."

Bruno Walpoth understands this, as he has said in an interview, "My sculptures do not tell stories. Nor am I even attempting to transmit messages."

As a young man C. S. Lewis craved something he called "northernness," an area that hovered due north of England, situated precariously between ocean and sky, shot through with oxygen and those famous northern lights. It was more than just a geographic location for he had no desire to travel past the Faroe Islands through the Norwegian Sea, Greenland Sea, Arctic Ocean, to the Arctic Circle, replacing his imagined territory with factual ice floes and polar bears. This was not a desire for somewhere in the past or somewhere that had yet to exist. Its texture was severe, sad, deprived, and vaguely associated with time. His northernness existed for him alone and later, as an adult, in the union with God in heaven, "sweeter than the fulfillment of any other human desire." Only in heaven, he believed, does there exist an immaculately tailored, one-of-a-kind response to the unnamed longing in each of us.

"You have stood before some landscape, which seems to embody what you have been looking for all your life," wrote Lewis in *The Problem of Pain*, "and then turned to the friend at your side who appears to be seeing what you saw—but at the first words a gulf yawns between you, and you realize that this landscape means something totally different to him, that he is pursuing an alien vision and cares nothing for the ineffable suggestion by which you are transported. . . . All the things that have deeply possessed your soul have been but hints of it—tantalizing glimpses, promises never quite fulfilled, echoes that died away just as they caught your ear. But if it should really become manifest—if there ever came an echo that did not die away but swelled into the sound itself—you would know it. Beyond all possibility of doubt you would say, 'Here at last is the thing I was made for.'"

The scent of cow shit mixed with hay triggers the hologram of a small hut, where aluminum milk jugs are stacked and pitchforks lean against the rough brown siding. I know that smell with my whole body. It won't be long before the actual huts slide into view, perched precariously on hillsides amid patches of snow melting quickly in the April sunshine. The train we're riding in decelerates as it climbs into Brünig, last stop before we enter the Hasliberg. I lower the compartment window, pull my teenaged daughter over so she can see what I saw the very first time when I was her age. Wet, coal-black tunnels breaking into bright hillsides covered with small yellow and white flowers. A mountain face so close we might skin our knuckles. The picture-perfect city of Lungern, its whitewashed, 110-year-old church ruling one end of the lake, casting steeple-shaped shadows onto the aquamarine waters.

"Wow, Mom," she says, "it's really beautiful."

Sensual experiences, like the basso peal of cowbells or sun-blindness on a ski slope are remembered in the body over an extended period of time. You don't exactly secure these things on a drive-by over a mountain pass. Meaning and sentiment accrete slowly and steadily. Every shack, trail, trickle of water tells a story. What did I expect her to say, this girl doing her best to sound matter-of-fact.

Worse, I start to cry, which sets off her squirm of embarrassment. I try to explain the flow of heat around my heart that migrates into my throat that doesn't exactly signal *happiness* at the sight of my beloved mountains and lakes. We're just arriving and have a full month to look forward to, but I'm constantly nudged by time, acutely aware how fast an hour, day, week progresses when we'll have to return home, *real* home, with its tangle of introduced species, repetitive grocery lists, and predawn radio alarm clocks. What is present consciousness except a keyhole through which the future flows into the past?

Oh golden town of Goldern. So gorgeous you can hardly stuff it in your eyes. A cross between the brothers Grimm and Disney, but the girl doesn't lose her parents to an ogre nor does she grow up to marry a handsome prince who falls in love instantly and whisks her off to a castle to live happily ever after. The more I speak, the more disgusted my daughter becomes, till finally I have to admit this is a secret I should never have revealed to anyone, even her. I'm one of those sad sacks who cannot describe happiness within an ounce of accuracy, let alone appreciate it. I'd traveled four thousand miles to revisit this country, minutes away from the specific scene of my longing, and now I feel more deeply bereft than ever.

Maybe I had a centuries-old life here. I learned the language easily, ravenous, with near perfect accent. For me, the occasional whiff of PostBus exhaust is a beloved, glorious fragrance and I breathe deeply as if I were standing next to the sea. I'll never have enough meticulously stacked woodpiles, switchbacks through conifers, formidable granite jutting into the skyline, for they are the anchors of my *Fernweh* (far-sickness) *and* my Heimweh. This is home, mother, heaven. In my version of Sehnsucht too, the want for a place is inextricably tied to its loss, and joy cannot be meaningful unless it contains a full helping of its opposite, despair. The Swiss Alps were not the first mountains I ever saw, but they imprinted, such that any landscape was never impressive enough unless there were serious peaks, like these. They created a concave area in my brain, a mold that fit precisely the real Wetterhorn above the Haslital and I spent the rest of my dreaming life trying to jigger the two sets together.

Councilor Blocher backs away from the podium, the next appointment urging him to move on, catch that train back to Bern. He turns his hands palms up to welcome artists, visitors, and the people of Brienz, who break from their polite attention and meander between the sculptures. Some will shrug their shoulders. Others shade their eyes, as if the moment is too intimate and they want to put distance between themselves and the art. Still others will increase that distance by murmuring evaluations or judgments.

They all appear slightly unsettled by the artist's sober attempt to make visible the invisible, for it may be impossible not only in wood but in paint, clay, music, literature, silent prayer, or indeed any human expression.

How to Return

The trip home is a physical weaning off the drug "mountain-land." The train travels in one direction—down, brakes squealing through corners and damp tunnels where rock glistens barely two feet away from your face pressed to the closed window. Closed, yes, because the conductor watches closely, though pretending to adjust her satchel. Six minutes to make your connection in Lucerne is no problem when you know the platform number: *Sechs*. Six. No need to verify the overhead schedule though you can hear its digits chattering. Then onward inside the well-mannered express train direct to Zurich *Flughafen*. The only struggle is tethering your bags, which have a mind of their own on the slick flooring. Thank goodness for an Indian gentleman who throws out his leg just in time as the train tilts through a turn.

Still a long way from home, but inching closer, or inching away from your real home, which is it? Is there the possibility of two homes? The one you live in and the one your heart belongs to? Mown into the grass on a trackside hill is a heart, yes a heart, too serendipitous and corny to believe. At its center a wooden fox is poised for the kill, nose and tail lined up like an arrow, but the only thing killing you is your withdrawal from this land. *I'm sad, mama, can you hear me?*

And where is your mother now? Where are your Ecole parents, Armin and Natalie, who died within a year of each other? Three of their adult children deliver three different answers: Molly defers to Piet. Piet defers to his father's wishes that the location of their ashes remain secret— Armin did not want a series of visitations, as if he were some celebrity or reincarnation of Buddha. Chris tells the story of Armin's journey on the *camino* to Santiago de Compostella, how he longed to repeat the experience but was held back by family exigencies. In the end, Chris took the pilgrimage himself and, arriving at the shrine of the apostle St. James, threw out a handful of *Vater*, just as Vater had desired.

Natalie asked for the ocean, the Atlantic lapping the shores of her Rhode Island, but after her death this seemed like a long way to travel. Thus her ashes were strewn below a Hasliberg footbridge over a shall-remain-nameless brook, where a small rockslide had taken place, the unstable spot roped off with red and white tape to warn hikers. *Mutter* will find her way to the Aare, then the Rhein, North Sea, and maybe the Atlantic, for as we know all waters are connected and all parents live on in the hearts and minds of their children.

Or do they? We lose a beloved mother or teacher or sister or best friend; we move away from a beloved country and yes have to bear it, for no such space can be adequately filled. The absence itself is what we are given, preserving our connection with the lost, though it feels so peculiar and yes it hurts.

A chime sounds, a sultry voice announces: "*Wir kommen in Zürich Flughafen an. Endstation.*" Everyone off the train! You'll notice the pace here has seriously picked up. Once you've set foot on the platform, the Swiss just want to scuttle you along as efficiently as possible. Simple enough to find your gate perhaps but don't stand still and don't miss a turn or you'll enter a whirligig of corridors and overhead signage, expensive duty-free shops, and security guards toting real machine guns. This is not yet your mother's house even if she were alive. It is a bustling hub on the edge of a crowded city with citizens from all eras and countries packed like hardware store paint samples into one infernal time zone. Every shade of blond, every skin tone from deep Africa to winter Norway. Someone clips your anklebone with his hard-shell suitcase but you are slow to react and he's too far ahead for even a *Hey you. That was painful.*

Go pay for your little *Brötchen, Käse, Schokolade.* The woman at the cash register is eager to sort it all out and get on with the next customer and presumes you can't tell rappen from Franken. She reaches for your wallet. She reaches for your wallet! You're far away from the teenager who moved fluidly through these transactions, but you still have some chops and place in her hand exact change. Last chance to sift these coins, feel the weight of a five-franc piece, its girth and shine and long-ago buying power of twenty dollars. Current value is just five, but this too will change depending on the weather and economics and the passage of decades.

Hey you. I'm no tourist. I am someone who lived here and came to know this place, and the lessons I learned were not easy. Say you're sorry.

For the American teenager just shy of eighteen, there were a few options for the transatlantic journey home: freight ships that accepted passengers; inexpensive charter flights out of Germany, Iceland, or Spain; and commercial carriers, like Pan Am and TWA, but the queen of them all was Swiss Air—Florence Nightingale of the skies, angelic and ever so dear. Today, you are bumped off Delta 909 and, after staging a small fit, rescheduled first class to Kennedy. Swiss Air. Oh, the wide leather seats and dignified passengers. Oh, the pillows encased in crisp cotton. This is no nightmare-encrusted cruise ship flying just above water, no dilapidated aircraft, rust-eaten and barely navigable. A stewardess swishes by in red and white, exhaling a whiff of cinnamon. She lays an ivory napkin over your lap and a small tablecloth on your tray. From the tip of her ice tongs, she offers a steaming wash-cloth—"Go now and wash yourself first, for the sun will laugh at you if he sees how dirty you are." (*Heidi*)—then circulates with wine and champagne and of course you are of age, though no one is carding here. There's a little basket of brioche and chive-butter, lamb chops, and fingerling potatoes. A simple Bibb salad, and minutes later, chocolate mousse baked in its very own clay ramekin.

Tuck in your heels, pull the flannel blanket to your chin. Lay your pillow against the humming shell of the plane. . . .

And sleep. Four hours of dreamless sleep you sink into, without a twitch.

Acknowledgments

This book is a composite of research, memory, dream, interviews with real people, and a tincture of embellishment. The events, anecdotes, and characters are sifted through my art and thus do not always adhere to facts. Some of the names have been changed. I do not claim to speak for all of Switzerland, as my experience was confined to a small area of the Hasliberg, Bernese Oberland, Canton Bern.

My huge gratitude to K. C. Hill, Kathleen Hennessy, Mark Felsenthal, and Lüthi family members Piet, Chris, and Molly. Jürg Jucker was instrumental in allowing me access to Armin and Natalie's archives. Melissa Baggs, Sonia Benenson, Ashley Curtis, and Phillip and Marie-Anne Hostettler were most helpful in their conversations.

Above all, I can't thank my parents, Bill Gorham and Peg Morton (1929–1980), enough for giving me the extraordinary gift of this place, this school, these friends and teachers, this life-changing experience.

"The Not-So-Awful (Swiss) German Language" was first published in the *Normal School* (Spring 2016).

Sources

In Order of Relevance

Interview with Robert Stickgold, Nova, November 30, 2009, http://www.pbs
.org/wgbh/nova/body/stickgold-dreams.html.

The Scientific Study of Dreams, by G. William Domhoff, American
Psychological Association, 2003.

Dreaming: A Very Short Introduction, by J. Allan Hobson, Oxford University
Press, 2011.

The Dream Encyclopedia. James R. Lewis and Evelyn Dorothy Oliver, Visible
Ink Press, 2009.

"Letter from Paul Geheeb to Adolphe Ferrière," Schloss Greng, October 9,
1939, Paul Geheeb Archives.

The Politics of Progressive Education, by Dennis Shirley, Harvard University
Press, 1992.

The Future of Nostalgia, by Svetlana Boym, Basic Books, 2002.

A Tramp Abroad, by Mark Twain, American Publishing Company, 1880.

"The Longest German Word," by Hyde Flippo, 2016, http://german.about
.com/library/blwort_long.htm.

The Alpine Journal, a Record of Mountain Adventure and Scientific Observation,
by Sir Leslie Stephen, Douglas William Freshfield, Sir William Martin
Conway, Arthur John Butler, and other members of the Alpine Club;
Longmans, Green, Reader, and Dyer; 1874.

"The Aare Gorge," Swiss Department of Tourism, 2016, http://www
.myswitzerland.com/en-us/gorge-of-the-aare-meiringen.html.

"A Chilly Float down the Aare River in Bern, Switzerland," by Courtney
Davis. *Dallas Morning News*, August 28, 2010.

"Escaping the Endless Adolescence," by Joseph and Claudia Worrell Allen, *International Journal of Biometeorology*, 2007.

"Overshadowing the reminiscence bump," by Martin A. Conway and Shamsul Haque, *Journal of Adult Development*, 1999.

"Things Learned in Early Adulthood Are Remembered Best," by D. C. Rubin, T. A. Rahhal, L. W. Poon, *Memory and Cognition* 26, 1998.

"Emotionally Charged Autobiographical Memories across the Life Span," by D. Bernsten, *Psychology and Aging* 17, 2002.

"Generation Identity and the Reminiscence Bump," by A. Holmes and M. A. Conway, *Journal of Adult Development* 6, 1999.

"Why You Truly Never Leave High School," by Jennifer Senior, *New York Magazine*, January 20, 2013.

Parliamentary speech by Hans-Rudolf Merz, http://www.youtube.com /watch?v=E5agWxzWTsc, video by Beat Hochheuser, uploaded September 20, 2010.

"Just Once I'd Like to Be Accepted for Who I'm Not," by B. Mankoff, *New Yorker*, April 20, 2015.

Beyond Chocolate: Understanding Swiss Culture, by Margaret O. Davidson, Bergli Books, May 1, 2002.

Xenophobe's Guide to Switzerland, by Paul Bilton, Oval Books, 2008.

Wanderings among the High Alps, by Sir Alfred Wills, R. Bentley, 1858.

Peering over the Edge: The Philosophy of Mountaineering, edited by Mikel Vause, Mountain 'n Air Books, 2005.

Roderick Hudson, by Henry James, MacMillan, 1879.

La Place de la Suisse Concorde, by John McPhee, Farrar, Straus and Giroux, 1994.

"Aesthetic Preference for a Swiss Alpine Landscape: The Impact of Different Agricultural Land-Use with Different Biodiversity," by P. Lindemann-Matthies, R. Briege, B. Schüpbach, and X. Junge, *Landscape and Urban Planning* 98, no. 2 (2010).

CIA: *The World Factbook*, http://www.earthsendangered.com/searchregions3. asp?search=1&sgroup=allgroups&ID=564.

"When Desire Leads You up the Garden Path," speech by Federal Councilor Christian Bloch, July 10, 2006. http://www.ejpd.admin.ch /ejpd/en/home/aktuell/reden---interviews/reden/archiv/reden_christoph _blocher/2006/2006-07-10.html.

"Clive Staples Lewis," by Helen Gardner, Proceedings of the British Academy, 1965.

Passages from the Ecole D'Humanité's philosophy and mission are drawn from its brochures, website (http://www.ecole.ch/), and other recruiting materials.

Illustration Credits